New
Techniques

The Grand Tour

New Techniques

Flavio Conti

Translated by Patrick Creagh

HBJ Press
a subsidiary of Harcourt Brace Jovanovich, Inc.
Boston

HBJ Press

President, Robert J. George

Publisher, Giles Kemp

Vice President, Richard S. Perkins, Jr.

Managing Director, Valerie S. Hopkins

Executive Editor, Marcia Heath

Series Editor, Carolyn Hall

Staff Editor, Chris Heath

Text Editors: Jack Beatty, John Bennet, Leonard Bushkoff, Elizabeth S. Duvall, Joyce Milton

Editorial Production: Karen E. English, Ann McGrath, Eric Brus, Betsie Brownell, Patricia Leal, Pamela George

Project Coordinator, Linda S. Behrens

Business Manager, Richard White

Marketing Director, John R. Whitman

Public Relations, Janet Schotta

Business Staff: Pamela Herlich, Joan Kenney

Architectural Consultant, Dennis J. DeWitt

Text Consultants: Janet Adams, Perween Hasan, James Weirick

Design Implementation, Designworks

Rizzoli Editore

Authors of the Italian Edition: Dr .Flavio Conti, Giorgio Morano, G. M. Tabarelli, Gabriella Porta, Daniele Riva, Bruna Vielmi

Idea and Realization, Harry C. Lindinger

General Supervisor, Luigi U. Re

Graphic Designer, Gerry Valsecchi

Coordinator, Vilma Maggioni

Editorial Supervisor, Gianfranco Malafarina

Research Organizer, Germano Facetti

U.S. Edition Coordinator, Natalie Danesi Murray

Photography Credits:

Aerofilms: pp. 10–11 / *Aéroport de Paris:* p. 137 / *Alfieri & Bini:* p. 63 bottom right, p. 67 center left / *Almasy:* p. 143 bottom right / *Behnish:* p. 158 center left, p. 159 bottom left and right / *British Petroleum:* pp. 121–132 / *Cauchetier:* pp. 26–27, p. 28 top and center, pp. 30–35, p. 57, p. 62, p. 63 top, pp. 138–139, p. 140 center, bottom left and right, pp. 141–142, p. 143 top and bottom left, pp. 144–145, p. 146 bottom left and right, pp. 147–148 / *Costa:* p. 25, p. 36 / *Hassmann:* p. 12 bottom, pp. 13–20, pp. 41–52, p. 153, p. 156 bottom left, center, and right, p. 157, p. 158 top left and right, bottom left and right, p. 159 top, p. 160, p. 161 left and bottom right, pp. 162–163 / *Klammet & Aberl:* pp. 154–155, p. 156 top / *Magnum-Freed:* p. 28 bottom / *Magnum-Hess:* p. 161 top right / *Magnum-Hopker:* p. 164 / *Magnum-Lessing:* p. 146 top / *Rizzoli-Müller:* pp. 73–84 / *Scala-Scarfiotti:* p. 68 / *SEF:* p. 29, p. 63 bottom left / *Sheridan:* p. 9, p. 12 top, pp. 58–61, pp. 64–66, p. 67 top left and right, bottom left and right / *Sipa-Press & Beutter:* p. 140 top / *Visalli:* pp. 89–100, pp. 105–116.

Library of Congress Catalog Card Number: 78-19239
ISBN: 0-15-003732-5

Printed in Hong Kong by Mandarin Publishers Limited

Contents

Preface
New Techniques

Two thousand years ago the Roman architect, engineer, and author Vitruvius expressed the hope that posterity would honor his name. His desire has certainly been realized, although perhaps not in the way he would have preferred. His ten-volume treatise, *De Architectura,* is the chief authority on Classical architecture. Far more famous, however, is his succinct definition of architecture as a synthesis of *firmitas, utilitas, venustas* or, roughly translated, "stability, utility, and beauty."

Others have formulated their own definitions of architecture, but most architectural theory has been a response to this ancient formula of Vitruvius. Indeed, the relationship between his three criteria has been vigorously debated down to the present day. Every age has its own preference and scale of values, and moreover, every age defines the meanings of the concepts in its own terms. For example, the idea of what constitutes beauty in architecture has ranged from the decorative enrichment of a Baroque palace to the integral mathematical harmony of a modern skyscraper or building by Le Corbusier.

Engineering, technology, and mathematics constitute, in one sense, the least poetic dimension of architecture, but they are vital to the creation of beautiful buildings. Le Corbusier always championed the cause of engineers, defining their role in the following way: "The engineer, inspired by the law of economy and led by

mathematical calculations, puts us in accord with the laws of the universe. He achieves an order which is a pure creation of his spirit . . . it is then that we experience beauty." The talent and practical ability of the engineer, and not least his development of new techniques, continually define new limits of architecture, making possible buildings and constructions that previously seemed impossible. And new techniques alter not only our idea of the potential of architecture but also our conception of beauty itself. Thus in the twentieth century, we have developed the technology needed to build an offshore oil-production platform and, in so doing, have created a technical marvel that has a beauty of its own.

Motives for attempting to overcome the limitations of existing techniques are many and varied. Sometimes, centuries after the fact, they are no longer known. Such is the case with Stonehenge, the mysterious circle of dolmens dating from prehistoric times, standing isolated on Salisbury Plain in southern England. These stones seem to have been connected with the worship of the sun and used as a huge astronomical observatory and calendar. Quite apart from the sophisticated calculations this required, transporting and erecting the great stones was in itself an extraordinary feat. Many of the stones were carried over long distances by the ancient Britons. With the aid of what is

believed to have been a platform of logs, they were able to construct the familiar post and lintel formations that have stood enigmatically on that windswept plain for 4,000 years.

The architect of the Pont du Gard is another unknown. In all probability he was a Roman military engineer who was called upon to perform the rather routine task of building an aqueduct to supply water to the flourishing Roman colony of Nemausus, modern-day Nîmes, in the south of France. Yet he was without doubt an engineer of remarkable ability. His aqueduct consists of three tiers of arches—the lower two are fitted together without mortar—which were skillfully assembled on site with a system of cranes and winches. The unadorned, rhythmic simplicity of the structure, which spans the gorge of the River Gard, makes it not only a supreme example of engineering but also a harmonious architectural achievement.

The anonymous builder of the medieval *stavkirke,* or stave church, at Urnes in Norway was more craftsman than engineer. The Urnes stavkirke is a testimony to the durability, versatility, and texture of a single material. The structure is constructed entirely of wood, from the spire to the floor, including walls, beams, pews, even nails. Recalling the seafaring Viking heritage of its builders, the stavkirke of Urnes stands in harmony with its rural setting, the spiritual center of a quiet hamlet overlooking the tranquil waters of the Sogne Fjord.

The Eiffel Tower seems a far cry from the stavkirker of Norway, yet there are some intriguing parallels between them. Both exploit the properties of iron and wood respectively. But while the little church of Urnes is a Christian temple, the Eiffel Tower is a secular one, typical of the age of positivism and the triumph of science. It stands on the threshold of an era in which techniques of applied engineering in architecture are about to transcend all previous limitations. Although the "300-meter tower" was supposed to have been pulled down after the Exposition of 1889, it found its way into the hearts of Parisians, and its lanky silhouette is now firmly established throughout the world as the symbol of the city.

The Panama Canal belongs to this same era of eager optimism. As a feat of engineering, it is practically without peer. The boldness of its execution, however, exacted its price: a sensational scandal in France, a revolution in Colombia that resulted in the creation of the Republic of Panama, and not least, the deaths of tens of thousands who worked under a brutal sun in swamps infested with malarial mosquitoes. But the canal, slicing through the isthmus between North and South America, modified the economic geography of the world, permanently altering the relationships between coasts and continents. It certainly fulfills William Morris' idea of architecture: every modification made by man to the surface of the earth to meet his needs.

The gigantic Hoover Dam, constructed in the 1930s on the Colorado River, is an equally remarkable technological achievement which has transformed the order of nature. The dam harnesses the waters of the Colorado, supplying vast areas of the southwestern states with vital electric power and water and irrigating the desert and enabling it to support life. Its massive curving concrete wall, wedged between the sheer sides of Black Canyon, has an elegance and purity of line which make it the prototype of the "utilitarian architecture" of modern landscapes.

Such constructions—dams, silos, mills, power stations, and dockyards—are now familiar landmarks. The most recent, and in many ways the most fascinating, among them are the production platforms which extract oil from under the ocean floor. These towers are certainly the ultimate test of the technological skills and inventiveness of their designers. Like so many technological advances, they are the children of fear: the fear of a civilization that looks on as its vital resources dwindle and disappear. So crews of engineers and workers have overcome the seemingly insurmountable problems of building platforms like *Graythorp I* in the treacherous North Sea. Standing 400 feet below sea level, these sophisticated structures are subject to the most prohibitive weather and sea conditions in the world. In only twenty or thirty years, they will be obsolete. At that time, all oil in the North Sea—if not the world—will have been exhausted.

The fantastic Charles De Gaulle Airport at Roissy-en-France, the third airport serving Paris, has already "processed" millions of passengers through its completed terminal. This massive gray complex is typically French in its logic and rationality. The airport consists of a circular terminal, providing centralized facilities and services, surrounded by satellite terminals where travelers board and disembark from planes. Among the airport's many innovations is its pedestrian circulation system. Instead of elevators and escalators, six transparent tubes pipe passengers across the glassed atrium in the middle of the doughnut-shaped central terminal, while fountains play below. De Gaulle is an example of modern architecture at its best: avant-garde and exciting, but not overwhelming and alienating.

More innovative still are the Olympia Park stadiums in Munich, which were erected for the Olympic games of 1972. The whole Olympic Village was built and landscaped at astronomical expense. Each of the three stadiums was united by Frei Otto's controversial tent-roofs which received more than their fair share of rebuke. His roofs, composed of steel cable netting covered with a skin of translucent acrylic, were intended as a deliberate symbol of advanced technology, a demonstration to the world of German technical superiority and, by extension, of German political rehabilitation after the militaristic 1936 Berlin Olympics. It is too early to tell whether Otto's roofs, which are guaranteed to last only fifteen years, represent a dead end or a milestone in the history of architecture. In any case, they were inspired by a bold and imaginative gesture.

In contrast, New York's Lever House, which opened its doors in 1952, now seems prosaic. Countless similar steel and glass towers fill the cities of the world. But Lever House is both a prototype and a symbol of twentieth-century architecture. Its architects, Skidmore, Owings and Merrill, exploited all the techniques and developments available to modern design, producing a streamlined, elegantly functional office building which also showed a respectful consideration for its thousands of human occupants.

If Lever House has been so widely imitated, it is to the credit both of the first-class professionalism of its designers and to those who recognized and appreciated its value as architecture. SOM extended the boundaries of architecture with a functional, aesthetically pleasing design. Other more innovative designs and techniques have proved less practical, less adaptable to daily working routines. Nevertheless, any work of art that goes beyond existing boundaries extends our horizons and brings us face to face with the future. It also stirs our sensibilities, broadens our notion of the beautiful, and lingers in the mind long after it is no longer in sight.

Stonehenge

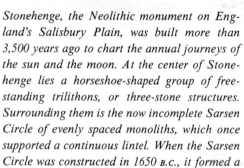

Stonehenge, the Neolithic monument on England's Salisbury Plain, was built more than 3,500 years ago to chart the annual journeys of the sun and the moon. At the center of Stonehenge lies a horseshoe-shaped group of free-standing trilithons, or three-stone structures. Surrounding them is the now incomplete Sarsen Circle of evenly spaced monoliths, which once supported a continuous lintel. When the Sarsen Circle was constructed in 1650 B.C., it formed a complete enclosure. The outlying partial circle of white chalk marks (preceding page) designates some of the fifty-six Aubrey Holes, which were used by ancient priests to help them predict eclipses. The Heel Stone (above), one of the oldest objects in the area, was placed 256 feet away from the center of the site. Its alignment with the rising midsummer sun was the key to the first truly scientific attempts to decode Stonehenge.

The great trilithons (background, above and near right) range from seventeen to twenty-two feet tall. Once carefully smoothed and polished, they are now eroded by wind and rust. Some of the defacement, however, has been at the hands of souvenir-hunting tourists. In fact, enterprising nineteenth-century guides even rented small hammers to those who had neglected to bring their own. The deeply eroded thirteen-and-a-half-foot monolith (left) is part of the Sarsen Circle. The name Sarsen, probably a corruption of "saracen," reflects the popular belief that the limestone rock used in the circle was of exotic origin; in fact, it was quarried twenty miles away. Far right, top to bottom, examples of the post and lintel construction at Stonehenge. The stones are held in place by hemispherical tenons on the tops of the upright stones which fit into mortices, or pockets, on the undersides of the horizontal lintels.

Following page, the rising sun breaking through the standing stones of the Sarsen Circle. Computer studies have shown that in the eighteenth century B.C. the major solar and lunar events of the year could have been viewed through the uprights of the trilithons and the Sarsen Circle.

Many of the massive limestone slabs, which weigh up to fifty tons each, have toppled (below right). A few were re-erected in 1958. The Heel Stone (below near left) stands near a modern road. On clear midsummer mornings the sun rises directly behind it on the northeast horizon. Above and below, protruding tenons atop upright stone slabs which once held the lintel of a trilithon in place. The bluestone slabs (above right)—found between the Sarsen Circle and the trilithons—were transported by sledge and raft from the Prescelly Mountains in Wales.

Following page, the morning sun over the Sarsen Circle. During the Middle Ages, these stones were known more poetically as the "Dance of the Giants." Stonehenge now attracts 700,000 visitors a year, and some members of a modern "druid" cult still worship within the shadows of the mighty monoliths.

Stonehenge England

Every year, a small band of white-robed "druids" converges on Salisbury Plain in southern England to celebrate the moment when the midsummer sun rises in direct alignment with a single, freestanding stone. Accompanied by harps, the worshipers begin their solemn incantation, waving bows of oak leaves and chanting, "Arise O sun, arise."

For many of the onlookers, only an occasional glimpse of sneaker-shod feet under the celebrants' white robes destroys the illusion that this is a truly ancient ceremony. In fact, these rites are staged annually at England's enigmatic prehistoric monument, Stonehenge, by a group that calls itself the "Most Ancient Order of Druids." The veneration these latter-day "druids" hold for Stonehenge—a reverence so deep that some cult members have won permission to have their cremated remains buried there—places them in the spiritual tradition of the monument's long-ago builders. Though fervent, they have no authentic connection with either the site or their own purported predecessors. Further, in perpetuating the notion that the original builders were indeed the real druids—learned priests of the ancient Celts—today's worshipers do history a grave disservice.

To this day, very little is known of the people who built Stonehenge. They belong to an age that predates not only the written history of the area but also the oral traditions of the Celts and Britons. Medieval Englishmen, however, had no way of knowing this, and their attempts to explain the monument drew on the legends surrounding the heroic Arthurian age. The most appealing story about Stonehenge is one of the oldest, set down by Geoffrey of Monmouth in his twelfth-century history of England's monarchy. According to this account, the true name of Stonehenge is "Dance of the Giants," and the entire complex was transported from Ireland to Salisbury by the wizard Merlin to mark the spot where a band of British soldiers had been ambushed by Saxons.

This association with Merlin delighted generations of poets, including the Elizabethans Edmund Spenser and Michael Drayton. Even leaving aside all questions of wizardry, less romantic souls were skeptical of these Arthurian associations—but for the wrong reasons. The Merlin story, if based on fact, would have placed the erection of the stones in about the fifth century A.D., and the skeptics did not think that a civilization as primitive as the ancient Britons could be responsible for such a substantial monument.

In the early seventeenth century, King James I invited the well-traveled architect Inigo Jones to investigate Stonehenge and solve the mystery. Jones theorized that the monument was actually a Roman temple. He substantiated his hypothesis by producing a series of drawings showing how the "temple" would look if it were restored. After Jones' death, his son-in-law John Webb published a book written by Jones which expounded at length on the Classical origins of Stonehenge. In retrospect, it is hard to comprehend how this idea could have been taken seriously. Perhaps Jones' reputation and a general awe of the accomplishments of the Romans lent an aura of credibility to the circumstantial evidence.

Those who championed another theory—that the pre-Roman druids were the builders of Stonehenge—were at least somewhat supported by science. John Aubrey, a seventeenth-century amateur antiquarian who drew meticulous sketches and charts of the site on behalf of Charles II, was the first observer to make a strong case for the druids. He did so entirely on the evidence of the stones themselves. Although he was ultimately proved wrong, Aubrey made an enormous contribution

This drawing by the seventeenth-century architect Inigo Jones exaggerated the already remarkable scale of Stonehenge. Jones claimed that it was the ruins of a Roman temple.

Below, a plan of the Sarsen Circle showing the location of both standing and fallen monoliths. Right, a plan of the entire site.

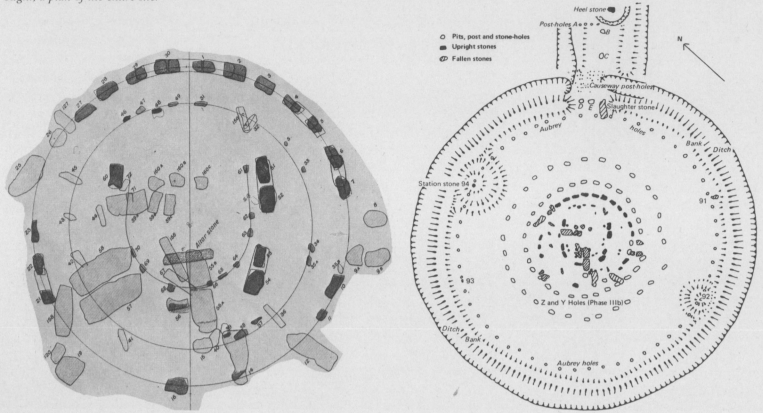

to future research by mapping the location of a circle of refilled holes running just inside a ditch that surrounds the site. There were fifty-six of these holes, averaging two and a half feet deep and filled with such debris as wood ash, flint flakes, and even some human remains. They are known to this day as the Aubrey Holes. Despite their systematic placement, no satisfactory explanation of the holes was advanced until the mid-1960s. Aubrey himself was quite modest about his discovery which would eventually become the key to solving the Stonehenge mystery, saying only, "I have brought it from an utter darkness to a thin mist."

The second great advocate of the druid hypothesis was Dr. William Stukeley. His book on Stonehenge, published in 1740, was both more scientific and more fanciful than Aubrey's. Stukeley was so enthralled by the mystique of druidism that he credited its priests with numerous magical powers and claimed to have found a link between them and the ancient Phoenicians. Nevertheless, his more imaginative conclusions were often extrapolated from his otherwise sound and perceptive obser-

vations. For example, Stukeley was the first to recognize the existence of the broad avenue flanked by ditches that runs from the main site to the River Avon several miles away. Based on its configuration, he reasoned that Stonehenge was a temple to a serpent god. The serpent was sheer whimsy, but in focusing attention on the avenue, which other observers had failed to note, Stukeley made an important contribution to our knowledge about Stonehenge.

Similarly, Stukeley was far ahead of his time in trying to arrive at a date for the construction of Stonehenge by scientifically analyzing internal evidence. He recognized, quite correctly, that "the principal line of the work, [points to] the northeast whereabouts the sun rises when the days are longest." Stukeley also determined that, by calculating the division between the orientation of the stones and the present position of the sun, it would be possible to establish their age. Unfortunately, his final calculations—based upon the erroneous assumption that the ancient builders had used a magnetic compass and some rather faulty logic—gave support to

the druid theory by placing the monument's construction in the year 460 B.C.

Modern scholars generally agree with Stukeley that the sun is the key to understanding Stonehenge. However, examination of tools and other objects found at the site indicates that Stukeley's dates were wrong by more than a millennium.

Stonehenge was actually built in three stages. The first, begun between 1900 and 1800 B.C., was the work of a late Neolithic people known to us as the Windmill Hill culture. The Aubrey Holes with their surrounding ditch and earthen bank were constructed during that time, and the single, freestanding rock called the Heel Stone was erected, although not in its present location. (The name Heel Stone derives from an apocryphal story that tells of the devil throwing this thirty-five-ton boulder at a poor friar who deflected it with his heel—leaving a mark in the stone that can still be seen today.) Whatever it meant to the Windmill Hill people, the Heel Stone was obviously considered to be significant even before it was moved to its later site in line with the rising midsummer sun.

Between 1750 and 1700 B.C., the second stage of construction was undertaken by another group, known to archaeologists as the Beaker people after their custom of burying pottery beakers in their graves. The Beaker people built the avenue as an approach road and began the construction of two concentric circles of five-ton bluestone rocks within the circle of Aubrey Holes. These circles—never quite completed—were later dismantled; but the mere act of bringing the stones to the site was sufficient to win the Beaker people a central place in the history of Stonehenge, for the stones were quarried over 240 miles away in the Prescelly Mountains of Wales and carried to the Salisbury Plain by sledge and raft. A re-creation of the journey, sponsored by the BBC in 1954, proved that this feat, though puzzling, was not beyond the capabilities of ordinary men.

The hulking silhouettes that now dominate the site of Stonehenge were the work of still another culture—the more advanced Wessex people. Beginning in about 1650 B.C., they raised five enormous trilithons, or three-stone figures, at the center of Stonehenge, forming a horseshoe that opened toward the northeast horizon. Each trilithon consisted of two closely placed, upright stones topped by a single lintel. Around these, they built a continuous post and lintel circle, ninety-four feet in circumference, which is known today as the Sarsen Circle. Sarsen, a name that may have derived from "saracen," refers to the type of limestone from which both the circle and the trilithons are made. Although the name reflects the belief of medieval observers that the stones must have been of exotic origin, they were actually quarried at Marlborough Downs about twenty miles away. Only sixteen uprights and five lintels of the Sarsen Circle remain standing today.

The so-called Slaughter Stone, a flat slab twenty-one feet long that is embedded along an imaginary line between the Heel Stone and the opening of the trilithon horseshoe, is also thought to date from the time of the Wessex people. Because of its name, visitors have often imagined—with no basis—that this stone was used for human sacrifice. Both the Slaughter Stone and the so-called Altar Stone, which lies within the trilithon horseshoe, continue to perplex scholars, some of whom suggest that the stones originally stood upright.

Most of the construction by the Wessex people was completed in one relatively short span. There were, however, two subsequent periods of building activity. In the first, two more circles of holes, now called the Y and Z circles, were dug between the Sarsen Circle and the Aubrey Holes. Modern excavators have found these holes to be filled with a puzzling array of debris, from human ashes to Iron Age implements as well as the litter of relatively

Many different solutions to the mystery of Stonehenge have been proposed. Among the theorists (left to right) were: Inigo Jones; Walter Charlton, who attributed it to the Danes; John Aubrey, the first champion of the druids; and Joseph Lockmeyer who, with astronomical calculations, was the first to correctly date the monument. Below, Jones's vision of a Roman Stonehenge.

recent visitors. Although the Y and Z circles are among the most recent additions to the Stonehenge complex, they are also the most mysterious. Unfortunately, they have not been marked as the Aubrey Holes have been and cannot be seen.

In a second and final stage of "remodeling," the bluestone boulders from the dismantled Beaker Age circles were used to form a horseshoe and circular ring within the Sarsen Circle. Today these configurations are also somewhat difficult to discern as many of the stones have been removed or destroyed over the centuries.

Archaeologists have been able to tell us a great deal about how and when Stonehenge was built, but they have not been as successful in fully explaining its purpose. The most exciting recent addition to our knowledge of Stonehenge has been the work of an English-born astronomer, Gerald Hawkins. Hawkins's book, *Stonehenge Decoded* (1965), outlines how he used a computer to carry out the kind of precise calculations similar to those first

Right, members of a contemporary "druid" cult gathering at Stonehenge to celebrate the summer solstice. William Stukeley's eighteenth-century conception of the druids (below) inspired many fanciful notions about their history and customs, including the rite of the serpent worship at Stonehenge (below right).

attempted by Dr. Stukeley. The results showed persuasively that Stonehenge is a sort of astronomical observatory and calendar. The great trilithons were arranged so that important celestial events, namely the extreme declinations of sunrise and moonrise, could be observed through their uprights. Accordingly, the Aubrey Holes could have formed a primitive computer or abacus. Perhaps by moving a set of stones around the circle, one move per year, ancient priests could predict the advent of solar and lunar eclipses. And the Y and Z holes may represent an attempt to improve upon this system, making it possible to forecast the month and day as well as the year of an eclipse.

Hawkins's findings show that the early inhabitants of the British Isles had much in common with other ancient civilizations that had a profound interest in celestial events. In addition, there is now evidence that the Wessex people were not entirely

isolated from the rest of the world. Egyptian trade beads, Baltic amber, and objects fashioned by Mediterranean goldsmiths have been unearthed in southern England. Archaeologists even believe that the Wessex people were trading with Mycenaean merchants at a time when Stonehenge was still young.

Nevertheless, decoding Stonehenge is not quite the same as demystifying it. On the contrary, every addition to our knowledge of its history raises new questions. Why, for example, did the Beaker people bring boulders all the way from Wales to build their stone circles? Was the Merlin legend, which has turned out to be closer to the truth than the theories of many well-educated students, a distillation of some folk memory that continued long after the death of the Wessex people? And if the rites of the druids were never practiced at Stonehenge, then what kind of rituals did take place there?

New theories about Stonehenge continue to appear every few years, but so far none has succeeded in completely dispelling the aura of inscrutability that surrounds this monument. Compared to the Egyptians and the Greeks, or even to the druids who left their legacy in myth and folklore, the preliterate cultures of southern England will probably always seem remote to us. Few of those who come to marvel and speculate at Stonehenge would dispute the judgment of Henry James who remarked that it "stands as lonely in history as it does on the great Plain."

Pont du Gard

Nîmes, France

The Pont du Gard—the famed bridge spanning the River Gard, a tributary of the Rhône in southern France—was built by the Romans around 19 B.C. and is part of an aqueduct that supplied water to the city of Nîmes, then called Nemausus. Its three arcades harmoniously complement one another, even though the arches on the two lower levels vary in span to accommodate the deepest channel of the River Gard in one instance and to restrict the number of piers within the flood plain in another. This slight irregularity is offset by the rhythmic regularity of the arch size of the uppermost tier. Today, the aqueduct is a link in a modern road which runs along the eastern side of the second arcade.

The two lower arcades of the Pont du Gard are made of dressed blocks, weighing as much as six tons each, fitted together without mortar. The angular shape of the piers, or cutwaters, was intended to prevent damage from swiftly moving flood waters. The largest arches of the aqueduct, those across the channel of the River Gard, stretch more than eighty feet, while the lowest level of the original bridge is about twenty-one feet wide. The third arcade, which carried the water channel, consists of thirty-five arches that are only ten feet wide. This 902-foot tier is constructed of concrete, covered in the usual Roman fashion with a thin stone facing. Concrete was also used to line the channel and protect it from leakage and erosion.

The conduit carried by the uppermost arcade (center right) is six feet deep and was covered with ten-foot slabs of stone to prevent evaporation and contamination of the water supply. The aqueduct originated in the region of Uzès and, after passing over the River Gard, continued another thirty-one miles to Nîmes through tunnels cut into the rock (bottom right). Tunneling was favored by the Romans because it protected the aqueduct from attack and was relatively easy to maintain.

Top right, a view downstream from the top of the aqueduct, 160 feet above the River Gard.

The slight gradient of this eerie water channel on the third arcade (left) allowed water to flow steadily. The rounded protrusions along the walls are calcium deposits, up to nineteen inches thick. Studies of the stratification of these deposits reveal that the aqueduct was in use until the ninth century.

Above, one of the piers of the second arcade. The projecting stones were deliberately left in place by the Roman builders so that they could support scaffolding.

The huge sandstone blocks of the Pont du Gard were cut from a nearby quarry and carefully prepared before they were hoisted into place by ropes and winches. Each stone was precisely squared at the site and then marked with a code indicating its placement on the bridge. For instance, a series of blocks found on the second arcade—ninth arch from the left—read FRS V, FRS VI, FRS VII, denoting that they are the fifth, sixth, and seventh stones belonging in the left front (fronte sinistra) of the arch. Today, the original Roman blocks show the effects of 2,000 years of erosion and neglect (right and above center). Restoration of the aqueduct was undertaken between 1843 and 1857; the cutwaters (left) provide a good comparison of Roman masonry and that of the eighteenth-century highway bridge.

Above right, the engraved name of "Le Nivernois," who visited the bridge in 1703. Many builders have recorded their names and the insignia of their trade—the hammer, chisel, and square—in the soft stone.

Pont du Gard Nîmes, France

During a visit to the south of France in 1878, the novelist Henry James was captivated by the monumental Roman aqueduct that spans the gorge of the River Gard. The Pont du Gard, he wrote, had "a kind of manly beauty, that of an object constructed not to please but to serve, and impressive simply from the scale on which it carries out this intention."

Built during the reign of Augustus Caesar, the Pont du Gard was part of a thirty-one-mile-long aqueduct which carried the waters of the Eure and Airan rivers from near the town of Uzès to the provincial city of Nemausus (modern-day Nîmes). It was probably constructed under the direction of Marcus Vipsanius Agrippa, governor of Gaul, who was also the water commissioner of the Roman Empire, and was completed around 19 B.C.

Although at that time the Romans possessed the most advanced knowledge of hydraulic engineering in the West, if not in the world, they were far from the first people to make use of aqueducts. Clay tablets describe water conduits in the Middle East as early as the tenth century B.C., and aqueducts were built in Abyssinia, Mesopotamia, Palestine, and Greece long before the Romans came to power.

But the Romans required especially vast quantities of water. Their cities were dotted with pools and fountains, from which citizens drew water for private use; labyrinthine public baths were popular Roman social centers; and the wealthy families who could afford the tax often piped water into their own homes. The overflow from the fountains and baths was ingeniously used to flush the city sewers. With so much demand, it is not surprising that it took eleven aqueducts to supply Rome itself with enough water for its three million inhabitants—about 350 million gallons a day.

Although the Romans were familiar with the mechanics of pumping, they preferred to build waterways using a constant downhill flow. This much simpler method eliminated the need for power and reduced maintenance to a minimum. At first, underground aqueducts were constructed in an attempt to protect the water supply from attack. As they were forced to find more distant sources, however, Roman engineers had to devise new methods to maintain the gravitational flow, and above-ground structures came to be used to carry water across valleys and ravines. Soon the Roman countryside was crisscrossed with great arcaded conduits, built by slave labor and maintained by a special division of the civil service.

As the empire expanded, its provincial centers adopted the customs of the capital, and aqueducts began to appear throughout Europe and the Mediterranean world. The flourishing provincial city of Nemausus, situated on the principal road from Italy to Spain, enjoyed the special favor of Augustus. There, the emperor established a legion of his soldiers, veterans of his Egyptian campaigns. By the time Agrippa made his second tour of the province, Nemausus had become one of its richest cities. The water supply, however, was fast proving inadequate, and within a few years a huge aqueduct was built to meet the city's needs. Most of that aqueduct runs underground, with the notable exception of the Pont du Gard, one of the city's finest architectural and historical treasures.

The Pont du Gard is built entirely of square blocks of sandstone, cut from a quarry only a few hundred yards upstream. Consisting of three tiers of arches of varying sizes and heights, the aqueduct rises 160 feet above the river. Its lowest

Right, an engraving (ca. 1750) by Giambattista Piranesi of the restored Aqua Virgo, built in Rome in A.D. 46. Common features of urban aqueducts included a dedication (A) and the rusticated stone facing around the arch (B). To again use the aqueduct, a superstructure (C) was later added atop the original construction.

The aqueduct of Pollio at Ephesus (above) was built during the reign of Augustus (below right). Others were later constructed at Aspendos in Asia Minor (right) and at Tarragona in Spain (below).

level is 467 feet long and about 21 feet wide. The now-incomplete uppermost series of arches, which carry the water channel, is 902 feet long and only 10 feet wide. The whole structure is supported in the rocky riverbed on huge piers, or cutwaters. These have an angular, boatlike shape in the front and back to strengthen the bridge against the rushing river and reduce erosion around the foundations.

The two lower series of arches were built without the use of mortar—a testimony to the remarkable precision of Roman stonecutting. The third level was built primarily of strong concrete faced with stone. This concrete, which also lines the water channel, has proved to be ex-

ceptionally durable. The water channel, barely five feet wide and about six feet high, is thickly lined with a cementlike calcium deposit. The channel is still partially enclosed by the ten-foot-long stone slabs that originally roofed the entire channel. This covering was built to prevent evaporation in the hot southern sun and to keep impurities out of the water.

The Romans managed to raise blocks weighing several tons to the height of the water channel, relying solely on men, mules, and oxen. By the time the aqueduct was being built, cranes and winches were already in use throughout the empire. A contemporary bas-relief shows a winch attached to an enormous hollow cylinder,

rather like a hamster's wheel, into which a number of men would climb. They would throw their weight from one bar to the next, causing the winch to turn and thus to lift the stones with a crane.

Other clever methods were devised to aid construction and maintain the aqueduct. Some of the carefully dressed blocks, for example, were deliberately left projecting out of the piers to serve as scaffolding supports should repairs be required. Great care was taken in both the preparation and the placement of the blocks to insure that they fitted snugly together. These blocks vary somewhat in size, as does the span of the arches of the two lower levels. (This latter variation results

The Pont du Gard was built at the direction of Agrippa (near right), son-in-law of the emperor. It was restored under Napoleon III (center), who was urged to do so by writer Prosper Mérimée (far right).

Below right, the aqueduct of Claudius (ca. A.D. 52) near Rome.

from the need to minimize the number of piers in the flood plain and to span the deepest river channel with a single arch.) These necessary inconsistencies, combined with the regularity of the top level's arches, maintain a dynamic overall rhythm throughout the Pont du Gard.

As Henry James noted, the Pont du Gard gains in beauty precisely because it so perfectly and economically fulfills its purpose. Using materials close at hand and foregoing any real ornamentation, the designer, who may have been an obscure military engineer named Veranius, created a monument in which technical excellence and architectural merit are perfectly married.

From the time of its construction shortly before the birth of Christ, the aqueduct that passed over the Pont du Gard continued to supply water to the reservoir in Nemausus. This Roman city reached its peak during the reign of the Emperor Antoninus Pius in the middle of the second century. Pools, fountains, and baths were fed by the reliable flow of water. The city continued to prosper until the fifth century, when successive waves of Vandals, Franks, and Visigoths invaded the region.

For many years it was thought that the aqueduct had been destroyed by the first of these invaders, but the layered calcium deposits on the bottom of the channel reveal a more probable history. When the Pont du Gard was in use, the little sediment that adhered to the channel formed a uniform depth along the length of the aqueduct. But when the water supply was cut off, the water remaining in the channel evaporated, leaving behind in certain places an unusually thick layer of sediment. Successive deposits of calcium indicate that the water supply was probably

cut during each siege of the city of Nîmes. Analysis of the deposits suggests that the aqueduct was most likely in use until the ninth century. It is believed that parts of the underground conduit, however, had been damaged before then.

By 858, the year in which Norman invaders completely sacked Nîmes, the city had declined from a great Roman metropolis of some 80,000 inhabitants to a small medieval town. Its few thousand residents could easily live by drawing water from wells and the great aqueduct was abandoned. Because it was no longer in use, it seems likely that peasants may have removed the relatively small blocks from the ends of the third tier of the Pont

du Gard for building materials.

Most of the Pont du Gard survived, however, just as it had held its own against the earlier invasions. But the bridge gradually fell into disrepair. Heavy use by pedestrians and their pack animals during the Middle Ages created even more serious problems. In the twelfth century, the Duc de Rohan, leading his men to the aid of a religious order in Nîmes, cut away one-third of each pier along the second level to allow for the passage of artillery. (It is indeed a tribute to Roman engineering that his amputations did not cause the collapse of the whole aqueduct.) In 1295, Raymond Gaucelin II, Lord of Uzès, was authorized to collect a toll, but none of this money was ever used to repair the bridge.

Over the centuries the need for a wider, safer bridge engendered much debate among the inhabitants of the city. Some felt that the Pont du Gard should be dismantled and a new road constructed in its place. Others were horrified by this plan, insisting that one of Nîmes's most beautiful antiquities must be respected. In the end, a compromise was reached. Between 1743 and 1747, a new bridge was built as an extension of the lowest arcade of the aqueduct, providing a convenient spot from which to view the monument as well as a new roadway connecting Nîmes with

Paris. The local populace was so pleased with this solution that a medal proclaiming *Nunc utilius,* ("Yet more useful") was struck in commemoration.

It was not until the reign of Napoleon III in the mid-nineteenth century, however, that the Pont du Gard received the attention it desperately needed. At the insistence of the writer Prosper Mérimée, who had been appointed inspector general of historical monuments in 1834 and who thought the bridge extraordinarily beautiful, a conscientious program of restoration was begun. Under the plan and direction of Charles Questel and Jean Charles

Laisné, this project was completed in 1857, and the Pont du Gard again began to enjoy the glory of former days. Twenty-one years later, Henry James stood on the banks of the Gard and confirmed the opinion of Mérimée: "The three tiers of the tremendous bridge . . . are unspeakably imposing, and nothing could well be more Roman. The hugeness, the solidity, the unexpectedness, the monumental rectitude of the whole thing leave you nothing to say. . . . You simply feel that it is noble and perfect, that it has the quality of greatness."

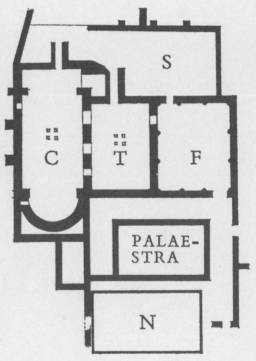

Above right, a plan of the Roman baths at Glanum in Gaul. In addition to the bath itself (N), such buildings included a gymnasium and hot (C), tepid (T), and cold (F) rooms. Above left, a vault in the baths at Gerasa in Palestine. Left, the latrine in the baths at Leptis Magna (Libya). Right, Roman bath accessories: a vial for oil, scrapers, and a spoon.

Preceding page, the little village and wooden church of Urnes, overlooking the serene waters of Norway's Sogne Fjord. From remote hamlets like this, the Viking longships once sailed to terrorize Europe and explore the uncharted North Atlantic.

In contrast to the stone churches of the towns, the stavkirke, or stave church, was essentially a rustic form, often constructed on the site of an earlier pagan shrine. Hundreds of these medieval wooden churches were erected in Scandinavia from the eleventh to the thirteenth centuries, but only about twenty now survive. Newly converted to Christianity, the Vikings incorporated elements reminiscent of the stone Romanesque architecture of Christian Europe into their own wooden "mast churches," in which the sophisticated woodworking of the longships is so evident. The first church at Urnes was built around A.D. 1060, when the great age of Viking exploration was already drawing to a close.

Most of the structure which survives today was constructed between 1100 and 1160; however, a door and carved panels from the eleventh-century building have been incorporated in the present church. Initially, the Urnes stavkirke had no west porch, although this one (left) was added soon after construction. The church was originally illuminated solely by the tiny, round, unglazed openings, still to be seen along the side wall between the two roof levels. The tower and small eastern apse (above and right) are the products of extensive seventeenth-century renovations of the building.

The Stavkirke of Urnes

Norway

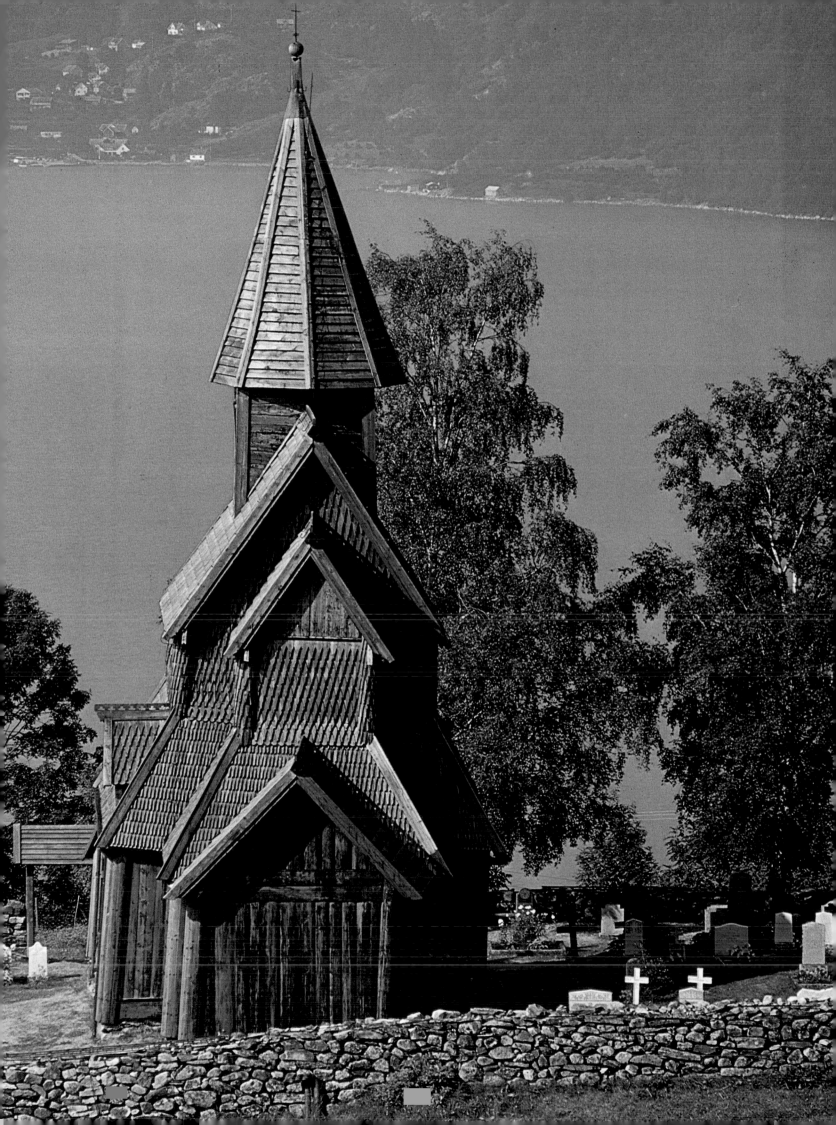

The nested pyramidal gables of the church are characteristic of stavkirke architecture (facing page). Sections of the roof define the different areas within the church: the nave, the choir, and the small apse. The church's north wall (below near left) is decorated with carved ornamental woodwork from the original structure.

Each shingle of the roof was hewn and shaped by hand (above and right). The wooden posts of the western porch (below right) are carved to resemble Romanesque stone columns. The bases of the columns are actually jointed to the groundsill. Although poorly preserved, the single decoratively carved capital of the western porch (below) retains some of the tendril-like forms of the so-called Urnes style of decoration. It was a variant of the much older "animal style" which had originated in central Asia and had later been highly developed in Scandinavia and Ireland, where it was used on reliquaries and shrines.

When a second front column and a corner column were cut out to make room for an extra pew, the Urnes stavkirke was greatly weakened—necessitating the diagonal brace which mars the interior today (above left and right). The small windows near the roof are reminiscent of ship portholes.

The rear gallery (below left) was erected during the early seventeenth-century renovation. Below, the medieval western door. Since metal was expensive and wood did the job, the twelfth-century stavkirke carpenters used metal only for the iron locks and hinges.

The ornamented pulpit, altar, rood screen, and left-hand pews date from the early seventeenth century and lend a Folk Baroque accent to the nave (right). Medieval taste survives a little more strongly in the chandelier. Originally, the dimly lit stavkirke interior was quite bare; most decorations were reserved for the exterior walls.

A candelabra in the form of a miniature Viking longship stands on the altar (above left). The theatrical seventeenth-century crucifixion scene above the altar contrasts vividly with the austere, twelfth-century Christ (above), which is above the entrance to the choir. The iron lock on the western door (far left) was fashioned by Norwegian craftsmen, while the candlestick (near left), made in Limoges, France, in about 1200, is one of the church's few imported treasures.

The varied motifs of the nave's wooden capitals include a bishop with his crozier (top right) and the interlaced zoomorphic and tendril forms of Viking tradition (center right). The much simpler woodwork on the pew ends (near right and far right) dates from the seventeenth-century renovations.

The Stavkirke of Urnes Norway

From the temptation of Eve to the Enlightenment of the Buddha, many of the major events in world religion and mythology have been symbolically associated with trees. But in the cosmology of the ancient Scandinavians, whose home fjords and valleys were rich in timber and poor in so much else, the tree assumed an especially profound and mystical significance.

Perhaps the most important of all Norse tree myths told of a mighty ash, called Yggdrasil, or the World Tree, which stood at the center of Asgard, the realm of the gods, and bound the whole cosmos together with its mighty roots. Yggdrasil gave protection and shelter, but it was also a reminder of the dark power of fate, for the tree's trunk was infested by rot, and only constant applications of the healing waters of the Spring of Fate could delay its

inevitable death. And when Yggdrasil toppled, the realms of god and man would be doomed.

Although the rest of medieval Europe may not have believed in the terrible significance of Yggdrasil, it was well acquainted with the destructive power that emanated from the Scandinavian forests. From the ninth through the eleventh centuries, bands of Scandinavian warriors poured south in their swift *drakkars,* or dragon-prowed longships, terrorizing the Continent with their daring raids. The eleventh-century chronicler Adam of Bremen referred to these invaders as "men of the ash," after the favored building material of their ships. History has come to know them as the Vikings. The word *vik* means "creek" or "inlet" in Swedish to this day.

Historians of the invaded countries

Above left, a schematic floor plan of the present Urnes stavkirke as it was originally built—without the western porch, but including a small, semicircular apse. Below left and center, interior elevations of the side and rear timber structure of the nave. They reveal an original clarity now obscured by the later modifications. Right, an artist's conception of the Urnes church of 1060, reconstructed from the surviving fragments. It indicates the more elaborate exterior decorations characteristic of earlier stave churches.

have left us with a widely accepted image of Viking brutality and depredation. As one Irish chronicler pronounced with anguish: "If there were a hundred iron heads on the one neck, each with a hundred sharp and indestructible metal tongues; and if each of them were to speak with a hundred clear and ineradicable voices; they would not suffice to tell how much the people of Ireland have suffered at the hands of this pagan, warlike and savage people." The Vikings' ruthless treatment of prisoners was harsh enough to shock an age all too accustomed to cruelty. The terrifying success of the Vikings resided in the intimate relationship between the longships and their crews. In the words of one historian, "The ships represented the peak of the technical ability of the Vikings. They were their instruments of power, their joy, their most treasured possessions.... What temples were for the Greeks, ships were for the Vikings."

But the outcries of the victims tell only

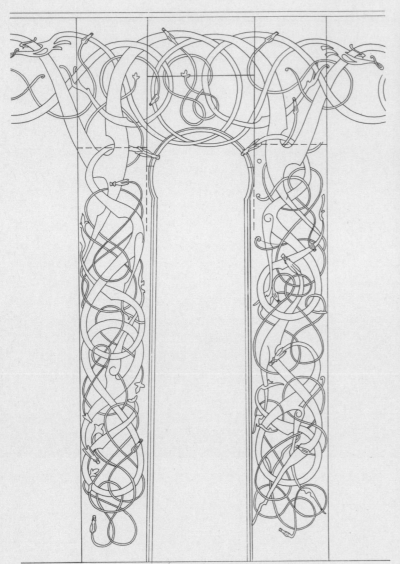

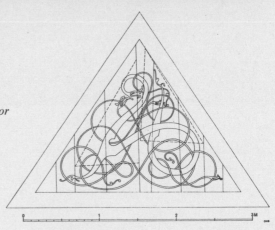

Urnes-style carved elements preserved in the present church include panels from the original church door and portal (above and left) and the eastern gable (right).

part of the story. The Norsemen excelled at trade as well as warfare, and they founded cities as well as destroyed them. Viking traders did business as far away as the Black Sea, and in Constantinople they served as the emperor's personal guard. In the year A.D. 860, the Slavs actually invited the Norsemen, whom they knew as the *rus,* to bring order into their chaotic lands. *Rus* chieftains accepted the offer, and as they did in Normandy and England, they stayed not to impose their will as conquerors but to become part of their adopted country.

The Vikings made no attempt to force their pagan beliefs on the people of other lands. They considered monasteries and churches fair targets for raids, but individual Viking chiefs also willingly submitted to baptism when they felt that it might improve their standing with foreigners. Eventually, these converted leaders intro-

duced the Christian religion into their homelands. Sweden welcomed its first Christian missionary as early as A.D. 823 but did not completely accept the new faith until three hundred years later, and according to Adam of Bremen, human sacrifice was still being practiced there in the middle of the eleventh century. The Danish king known as Harald Bluetooth was converted in A.D. 960 when, so the story goes, a priest named Poppo amazed the Danish court by grasping a white-hot iron glove and suffering no injury. But in fact, Harald Bluetooth and the Scandinavian kings who followed him were probably equally impressed by the advantages of belonging to the dominant religion in Europe.

Olaf Tryggvesson, the Norwegian ruler responsible for the conversion of Iceland, definitely used Christian missionaries to increase his own influence in that island's

factional politics. At home, he was less successful. When he died in A.D. 1000, his supposedly Christianized subjects reverted to paganism. A few years later, another King Olaf, later to become the patron saint of Norway, used rather unsaintly methods to persuade his subjects to change their faith. He offered them a choice between baptism and torture. Overwhelmingly, they opted for the holy sacrament.

Despite Olaf's success, the Scandinavians did not always comprehend that accepting Christianity was supposed to mean relinquishing everything associated with the old religion. Many Norwegians donned the cross while continuing to wear Thor's hammer, an amulet symbolizing the power of the Norse war god. And some had no difficulty in describing themselves as being of "mixed faith"—part Christian and part pagan.

This accommodation of both faiths was inevitably reflected in the architecture of Scandinavian churches, which commonly incorporated symbols borrowed from Norse mythology. But the influence of former beliefs went far beyond mere superficial decoration. When the Vikings began to build parish churches in large numbers—in Norway this occurred in the mid-eleventh century—they adapted native building methods and forms to the needs of Christian sacred architecture. The result was the *stavkirke,* or stave church.

Even the earliest stave churches display a level of sophistication that suggests they were based upon an existing style of wooden architecture. These conjectural antecedents may have been either pagan temples or earlier Northern European churches which are no longer extant. The form of the stavkirke changed little over three hundred years—from the mid-eleventh to the mid-fourteenth centuries. Unfortunately, most of these picturesque little churches were destroyed after the country converted to Protestantism, just as earlier pagan temples had been razed by Saint Olaf and his followers.

Today only about twenty-two stave churches remain in Norway—and far fewer in Sweden. Urnes is one of the better preserved examples of the form in an unspoiled rural setting. Parts of the stavkirke, including the interior furnishings, a small apse, and the tower, are the products of an extensive renovation undertaken in the early seventeenth century. But most of it dates from between 1100 and 1150 A.D. It is old by any standards, but for a wooden building it has survived to a remarkable age.

Even so, the present stavkirke is not the first constructed on this site. An earlier church, possibly the first of two, was erected in about 1060. Elaborately carved panels from the doorway and gables and a post were incorporated from this earlier building into the existing church. The intricate designs on these panels are based upon highly stylized four-legged animals entwined in serpentine and foliagelike forms.

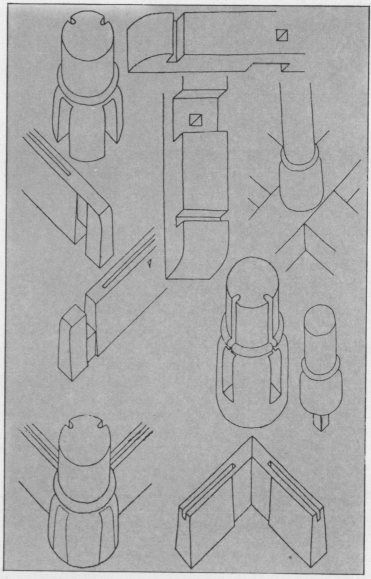

Although this Urnes-style design was refined by foreign influence, the motifs and methods are clearly drawn from the vigorous tradition of pre-Christian Viking art. The foliage may even be reminiscent of the legend of Yggdrasil, the World Tree, and the snakelike forms recall the Norse belief in a great serpent—the enemy of the gods of Asgard—who would emerge at the time of the gods' destruction. But whatever their precise significance, the Urnes-style motifs are evidently rooted in pagan beliefs.

The little church of Urnes could have been conceived and built only by a race of shipbuilders. The skill of the Vikings is evident in the sturdy, durable construction of the stavkirke, which survived centuries of savage winter storms. Even its visual impression reveals the seafaring heritage of its architects. Like a wooden ship, its exterior has been darkened and preserved over the centuries by applications of Stockholm tar.

The stavkirke takes its name from the vertical timbers which form its walls. The stavkirker were even known as "mast churches" because their columns resembled masts. Such stave construction is a more primitive form than the horizontal log construction found, for example, in the familiar American—and originally Scandinavian—log cabin. As with many religious structures, this archaic form may have been unconsciously retained out of a sense of tradition.

The walls of the church are of lesser structural importance than the rectangle of upright timbers that rises from a log base about three feet inside the main walls. These columns and the braces which connect them bear a superficial resemblance to the stone columns and arches of

Above and below right, cross sections through the more fully developed and preserved stavkirke in Borgund, Norway. Above right, a longitudinal section through another impressive stave church, showing the traditional dragonhead figures on the roof. This is now in an open-air museum in Lund, Sweden.

a Romanesque church. In fact, the Urnes carpenters did much to stress the similarity—carving bases and capitals on the columns and shaping the braces in the form of semicircular arches. Unlike most Romanesque churches, however, the row of columns which separates the nave from the sanctuary in the stavkirke makes the altar seem rather remote, more the private preserve of the minister than a focal point for the congregation.

The underlying principles of stavkirke architecture differ considerably from Romanesque churches. The arches of the former were not really load bearing, and in fact, not all of the many upright timbers were crucial to the support of the structure. As time went by the center post was typically cut off and left to hang in midair, as clearly was done in the construction of Urnes. Later at Urnes two more posts, one of them an important corner post, underwent further makeshift amputations and had to be braced when one family added a boxed pew. Thanks to the compensatory bracing, the structural integrity, if not the internal appearance of the church, re-

mains basically unharmed.

The stavkirke was wonderfully suited to the rigors of the northern climate. The false arches acted like knees knocking together, providing a degree of elasticity necessary in a country prone to fierce storms. A scholar who once took refuge from a particularly severe blizzard in the stavkirke at Borgund in Norway described how, after much creaking and groaning, the ancient timbers gradually took up the strain and the whole church bent with the wind like a great sailing ship weathering a

gale. Small wonder then that the carpenter-builders of the stavkirker often placed on their roofs, beside the Christian cross, carved dragonheads like those which once adorned the prows of Viking longships.

Although many of the stave churches, and especially those of western Norway, were erected under the aegis of local landowners, they were essentially a peasant form of architecture, scaled to their rural settings and built entirely of indigenous materials. Of course, the size of the stavkirker was limited by the length of the timbers available, and before long the cities and larger towns began to erect stone churches based on Continental models. The first of these cathedrals, built in Oslo, Hamar, and the Orkney Islands during the twelfth century, signaled a decline in the fortunes of Scandinavia. For better or for worse, the Vikings were ruggedly independent. They excelled at exploration and were able to coax a living out of lands that the rest of the world regarded as uninhabitable. But they lacked the natural resources, the political organization, and perhaps, the temperament, to compete with the major twelfth- and thirteenth-century centers of power—some of which they had helped to establish—either in warfare or in the building of cathedrals.

In the new era of better fortified towns and taller merchant vessels, even the Vikings' dragon-prowed ships became obsolete. The Scandinavians retreated to their home valleys to create a new kind of wooden temple, the stave church. There, the cross gradually triumphed over the drakkar-head. But the dark cosmology of Yggdrasil did not die easily. Pagan rites were still being practiced in remote parts of Scandinavia as late as the seventeenth century. In the words of Vilhelm Moberg, the Swedish author who was himself born into a poor rural family in 1898: ". . . the belief in fate has survived heathendom, providing an alternative explanation to Christianity of life's mystery. I have known many peasants who have declared their firm belief in a blind remorseless fate. . . . If anyone told them that their faith was originally the faith of the heathen, they would be deeply shocked."

Eiffel Tower

Paris

The Eiffel Tower, designed by the engineer Gustave Eiffel, was erected in the Champ-de-Mars for the Paris Exposition of 1889. The commissioners of the exposition hailed it a "masterpiece of French construction in metal," but not everyone agreed: Many notables, including Guy de Maupassant and Charles Gounod, vehemently denounced the tower, declaring it a national disgrace. Despite fears that the structure was unsafe, this monument to progress reigned as the tallest structure in the world for four decades, until the completion of New York's Chrysler Building in 1929. Today, nothing remains of the exhibition halls and pavilions which once filled the Champ-de-Mars parade grounds, but the controversial centerpiece of the fair—originally intended to stand for only twenty years—has become the popular, universally recognized symbol of Paris.

The tower consists of an iron framework supported on four "masonry" piers—which are, in fact, stuccoed and hollow, and contain the elevator lobbies. The real stone foundations extend some forty-five feet under the ground. Wide-angle photographs taken at ground level accentuate the tower's dramatic proportions. The sides of the base are almost one-half the height of the 984-foot tower.

The area enclosed by the legs of the tower covers more than two acres. Since the ironwork is prone to rust, the tower is painted every seven years. In recent times, its color has been changed from bronze to gray, but the paint is still slightly darker at the bottom than at the top to emphasize the height of the tower.

There are three platforms. The lowest, which houses a capacious and expensive restaurant, has sometimes been rented out for wedding ceremonies. The smallest platform, at a height of 903 feet, contains the private penthouse of the designer, Gustave Eiffel. He used it as an office and never actually lived there, although its original furnishings included a grand piano.

EIFFEL

Left, a memorial to the engineer Gustave Eiffel, dwarfed by the soaring iron girders of his most famous creation. The "300-meter tower," as the Eiffel Tower was first known, was a dream of nineteenth-century architects and builders who wanted to demonstrate the potential of metallic structures. Eiffel's design for the "dream" was heavily influenced by the problems presented by wind loads. Even in gales, the top of the tower sways no more than five inches. But from the start, Eiffel was determined that the tower would be acclaimed as an aesthetic as well as engineering triumph. In his own words: "I believe that the tower will have a beauty of its own."

Among the visible working parts of the Eiffel Tower are the elevator mechanism (above) and the open elevator cage (bottom left). The lamp (below) is one of a number of Art Deco fixtures added between the world wars. Other ornamental features include the fanciful restaurant sign (top near right) and arabesque ironwork details.

RESTAURANT

Eiffel Tower
Paris

thin, ridiculous profile of a factory chimney." But in the end the much vilified monument became the most visited attraction in Paris, a landmark that we now take for granted as the undisputed symbol of the city—the Eiffel Tower.

Gustave Eiffel's tower, as originally conceived, had no practical purpose. In fact, it was not even intended to be permanent. As the centerpiece of the fair, the Eiffel Tower was a novelty that was meant

Left, a caricature of Gustave Eiffel, which first appeared in a French newspaper. The Eiffel Tower became good copy for journalists. Le Figaro *even published an edition from the tower during the Paris Exposition of 1889. Below right, a comparison of the height of the tower with that of other monuments including the Great Pyramid, l'Arc de Triomphe, and St. Peter's Basilica.*

to enhance France's reputation in the eyes of international visitors and to show that France had successfully recovered from the Franco-Prussian War of 1870–1871.

The idea of a 1,000-foot tower had become almost an obsession among nineteenth-century engineers. As early as 1833, there was a proposal to build a tower 1,000 feet tall to celebrate the passage of the First Reform Act. The idea was raised again at the time of the 1851 Great Exhibition in London and, once more, on the occasion of the 1876 Centennial Exposition in Philadelphia. The idea also took hold in France where it was translated into the "300-meter tower."

The most dramatic opportunities to show off the potential of iron construction were presented by the great commercial and scientific expositions which proliferated in the second half of the nineteenth century. Facilities for such events were usually temporary but lavish, and the planners encouraged innovation. To modern eyes, the results were often more ghastly than inspired. Perhaps the most successful example of nineteenth-century exposition architecture was the first—Sir Joseph Paxton's Crystal Palace, a mammoth cast-iron and glass pavilion designed

When the Commission for the Paris Exposition of 1889 first announced plans for an iron pylon to straddle the fashionable gardens of the Champ-de-Mars, it created a storm of controversy. An outraged neighborhood association sued the municipal government for plotting "a crime against beauty." Three hundred leading intellectuals formed the "Committee of 300" to oppose the 300-meter tower and signed a petition protesting the "defacement" of Paris by this "barbaric mass" of exposed metal. Among the committee members was the writer Guy de Maupassant, who described the tower as a "giant and disgraceful skeleton with a base that seems made to bear a formidable cyclopean monument and which aborts into the

Left, the four foundations for one corner pier. They were begun in January of 1887. Work on the tower proper (below left) moved rapidly and was completed in just twenty-six months.

for London's Great Exhibition of 1851.

The Paris Exposition of 1889 was planned as a grand celebration of the centenary of the French Revolution, to be dominated by the 300-meter tower. Over 700 different designs for the tower were submitted. But the decision to award the commission to Gustave Eiffel was not unexpected. As early as 1884, Eiffel had drawn up plans for a tower for the imminent exposition, and the criteria laid down by the tower competition were based on his proposal.

Eiffel was one of the world's most experienced designers and builders of metal structures. He had dozens of bridges and aqueducts to his credit, including the 520-foot span of the Pia Maria Bridge in Portugal. Moreover, he was the designer of the steel skeleton of the Statue of Liberty.

Of all Eiffel's designs, the 300-meter tower was the most meticulously planned and executed. But Eiffel hoped that the tower would be considered an aesthetic as well as an engineering success. He belonged to the generation which regarded technology not just as a means to an end, but as a virtue in itself. In his own words, "The first principle of architectural beauty is that the essential lines of a construction be dictated by a perfect appropriateness to its line."

Many people, however, took comfort in the predictions of a leading Paris mathematician, who calculated that when the 700-foot mark was reached the mass of girders would collapse of its own weight. Once this danger point had passed without incident, the intellectual critics retreated to the position of the average Parisian who, all along, had merely shrugged his shoulders with a dismissive *"A quoi bon?"*—"What's the point of it?"

In any case, no amount of criticism could sway French officialdom from its chosen course. Edouard Lackroy, the Minister of Commerce and Chairman of the Exposition Commission, parried the protests of the intellectuals with the ironic suggestion that he would display their petition in a showcase at the foot of the finished tower. "Such fine and noble prose will be sure to attract crowds and perhaps even astonish them," he wrote. Of course, this was never done. But the tower itself disappointed no one in its power to attract visitors—as many as the Champ-de-Mars could possibly hold.

The Exposition of 1889 was, in some respects, an extremely bourgeois way to commemorate the French Revolution. Its opening ceremonies, on May 6 of that year, were boycotted by monarchist Frenchmen and by many foreign diplomats and invited dignitaries. Few European monarchs cared to join in celebrations honoring the centennial of a king's overthrow and execution. Nevertheless, the ironic consequence of the exposition was that Europe's aristocracy rediscovered the charms of Paris. The city, which had been shunned for two decades as a hotbed of radicals and Communards, was rehabilitated—in the eyes of the fashionable set at least as the city of boulevardiers, artists, and cancan dancers. The Belle Epoque had begun and Monsieur Eiffel's tower, illuminated every night by the brand-new invention the French called "the fairy electricity," was its beacon.

Not even Eiffel had imagined that the tower would become a permanent addition to the skyline of Paris. Originally, it was assumed that the structure would be demolished when the lease of the Société de la Tour Eiffel, a private investors' group, expired after twenty years. But after two decades, the tower had become an accepted Parisian landmark. It was still attracting a healthy stream of visitors and generating revenue for the city. But the

Above near right, workmen descending from a high riveting platform. Above far right, an official deputation hoisting the French flag at the summit on March 31, 1889. During the exposition, the Champ-de-Mars (right) was filled with pavilions and the other engineering wonder of the fair—the monumental glass and iron Hall of Machines.

threat of demolition probably spurred Eiffel to explore scientific and military uses for the monument.

On the most frivolous level, the tower was a constant source of amusement, a mecca for pranksters and eccentrics. One man climbed the staircase on his hands; another reached the first platform on stilts; and a third intrepid soul somehow managed to descend the 190 feet from the first platform on a bicycle. Much of this lighthearted experimentation was encouraged—even sought out—by Eiffel, who, in addition to his native scientific curiosity, was always on the lookout for ways

to prolong the life expectancy of the tower.

But the tower also attracted serious studies in the fields of meteorology and radio. In 1909, the Comte de Lambert pushed back the frontiers of French aviation by flying a Wright biplane over the top of it. Today, the tower houses government experimental stations which measure everything from meteorological conditions to radiation, but broadcasting is firmly established as its principal industry—next, of course, to tourism. Radio Tour Eiffel first went on the air after World War I, and in recent years a television transmitter has been placed atop the

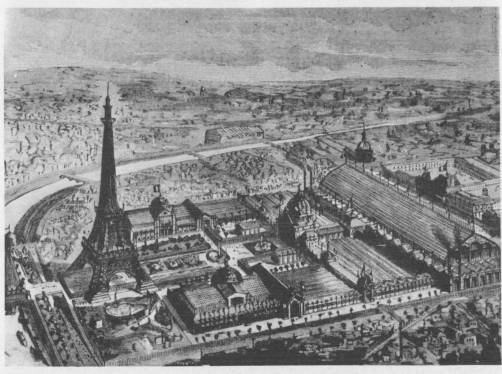

tower, adding some six feet to its original height.

For many years the dignified "old lady" was also the world's largest billboard. In 1925, during the Exposition des Arts Decoratifs, the tower was totally sheathed in graphic ornaments at a cost of half a million dollars. The lights were paid for by the Citroën company, in return for the inclusion of its name and trademark which appeared on the tower in illuminated letters ninety-eight feet high. The elaborate project required 375 miles of wiring to support the 250,000 lights in six colors which outlined the arches and silhouette of the tower. The spectacle could be seen from a distance of twenty-four miles.

Not all of the Eiffel Tower's history has been happy. Before protective barriers were placed around the observation platforms, the tower became a magnet for suicides. Then during World War II the Nazis occupied Paris and removed the French flag that traditionally flew from the tower's summit. A German threat to dismantle the monument was never carried out, but for years Parisians had to endure the sight of Nazi officers using the familiar landmark as a background for snapshots. These insults were finally avenged in the waning days of the occupation when four young Frenchmen boldly raced up the staircase of the tower and unfurled the tricolor once again. The liberation of the Eiffel Tower was considered too important to be left in the hands

Fair goers (above) on the third platform of the tower watch the firing of a cannon to mark the hour.

A powerful beacon and strings of electric lights, among the first in Paris, illuminated the tower during the festivities of the exposition (right).

of foreigners.

In retrospect, it is surprising how completely the hopes of Eiffel and the commissioners of the 1889 exposition have been vindicated. The tower has not only contributed to scientific progress in ways that they never could have envisioned, but it has also become the universally recognized symbol of Paris. Scores of painters, among them Seurat, Utrillo, Delaunay, and Dufy, have celebrated the Eiffel Tower in their works. Writers too—Apollinaire, Giradoux, Léon-Paul Fargue—found inspiration in the tower, as did film makers. René Clair produced a documentary entirely devoted to it, entitled *La Tour.*

If there has ever been a poet laureate of the Eiffel Tower, it was Jean Cocteau, the iconoclastic playwright and leader of the French avant-garde in the 1920s. Cocteau's first play, *The Wedding on the Eiffel Tower,* is set on the monument's first plat-

form and portrays two narrators in the roles of phonograph machines, an actor playing the part of an ostrich, and an orchestra playing noisemakers instead of instruments. During the play, one narrator reveals the significance of the setting with the words, "The Eiffel Tower is a world in itself. . . . It is the Notre Dame of the Left Bank."

The Eiffel Tower has become a repository of meaning for our era. Built entirely of iron, it is a monument to the optimistic Iron Age of the nineteenth century. But it represents much more than that. In the words of the French philosopher Roland Barthes: "Depending on our imagination, it becomes the symbol of Paris, of modernity, of communication, of science of the nineteenth century, a rocket, stem, derrick, phallus, lightning rod or insect. In the great domain of dreams, it is the inevitable sign. . . . It is impossible to flee this pure sign, for it means *everything.*"

Panama Canal

Panama

Preceding page, a Japanese container ship crosses Miraflores Lake in the early stages of its journey through the Panama Canal toward the Caribbean. To reach the lake, a ship must pass beneath the Thatcher Ferry Bridge (bottom left), which forms part of the Pan-American Highway, and along a channel to the Miraflores Locks (right and top left), where it is lifted to the level of the lake. At the end of the lake, the Pedro Miguel Locks (center left) raise it an additional thirty-one feet to the Gaillard Cut. This eight-mile trench, running through the Culebra Mountain, leads into Gatun Lake, a twenty-four-mile stretch of water which terminates in the Gatun Locks (above). Here the ship is lowered eighty-five feet to the level of the Atlantic. Another channel carries the ship past a protective breakwater and into Limón Bay. The entire trip from deep water to deep water takes about eight hours and covers 50.72 miles.

Near right, the control house of the Gatun Locks. Within, workers direct the operation of the locks by monitoring the valves which regulate the flow of water in the concrete lock chambers (above far right). Ships are drawn through the locks by four to twelve small electric locomotives called "mules" (top row). When a ship enters the lock chamber, enormous steel gates, seven feet thick and weighing up to 730 tons (far right), close behind it, and the water level is raised or lowered. After eight to twelve minutes, the ship passes out through another set of gates at the next level, either into a second chamber or out of the locks.

The Madden Dam (below) was built in 1934 to provide additional water reserves for the locks. Scarcity of water for the operation of the canal is a major problem during the dry season.

Although the largest supertankers and warships cannot make the passage, an average of 14,000 ocean-going vessels of every type and nationality use the Panama Canal each year, generating an annual revenue in tolls of about $145 million.

Above, a Russian freighter being boarded by a canal pilot, who will guide it through the waterway. Above left, a tug assisting a British bulk carrier in the Gaillard Cut. Below far left, a Japanese container ship in the Miraflores Locks. Below near left, two fishing boats traversing the canal.

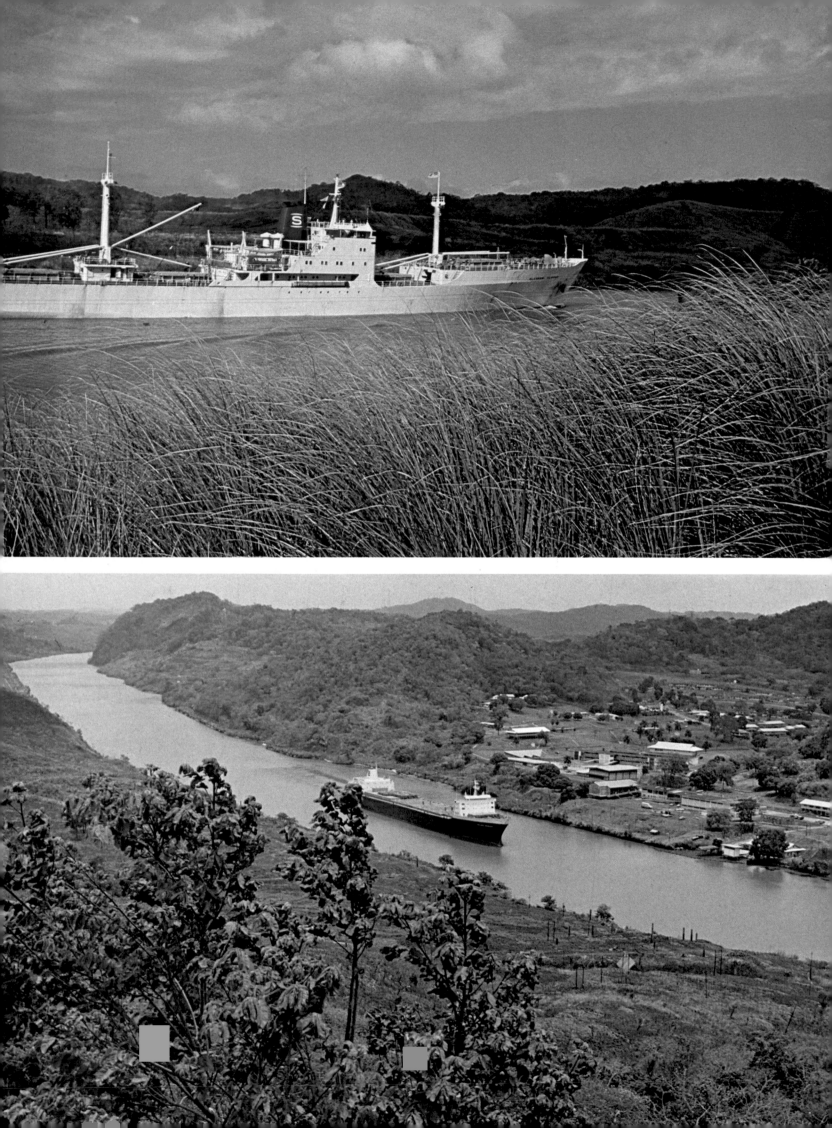

Right, a train on the Panama Railroad snaking its way across Gatun Lake. The railroad, completed in 1855, was an earlier solution to the problems of communications between the Atlantic and the Pacific. Without it, the canal could never have been constructed.

Left, two ships passing through the Gaillard Cut. Erosion in the cut, which measures 300 to 500 feet in width and at least 42 feet in depth, calls for continual dredging. The fast-growing tropical vegetation of Panama has also posed problems for the canal since its inception. During its construction, some 40,000 laborers died from malaria and yellow fever, carried by mosquitoes living in the surrounding swamps. Water hyacinths (below) would rapidly clog the canal if they were not cleared regularly.

Panama Canal
Panama

On September 25, 1513, a Castilian conquistador named Vasco Núñez de Balboa became the first European to cross the Isthmus of Panama and set eyes on the Pacific Ocean. For years European explorers—Amerigo Vespucci, Cortés, Pizarro, de Soto, and, of course, Columbus—had been searching the Central American coast for a waterway between the seas. Almost as soon as Balboa discovered the isthmus—only forty miles across at its narrowest point—plans were made to link the Atlantic and Pacific oceans. But nearly four centuries were to pass before the Panama Canal—"the Big Ditch," as it is often called—was finally completed.

In 1519, the Spanish government founded the town of Panama on the Pacific coast of the isthmus. It soon became the base for the conquest of the rich west coast of South America and the port from which the conquistadors shipped back to Spain the king's share of their treasure—his "royalty" of twenty percent.

Panama was only a short distance from Colón, the port on the Atlantic side of the isthmus, but travel between the two was treacherous. The route was not only mountainous but covered by thick tropical forests and swamps infested with poisonous snakes and malarial mosquitoes. By 1523, the first plan for a canal—to save both time and energy and reduce the risk of the trip—was presented to Emperor Charles V. But the technical problems of the project and the anticipated cost were formidable. The emperor, who was perpetually on the brink of bankruptcy, declared that "all the gold in the world would not suffice for such an undertaking," and the plan was shelved.

Throughout the eighteenth and early nineteenth centuries, however, European interests in a connecting waterway continued. In 1780, Lord Nelson, the great English admiral, unsuccessfully tried to seize the isthmus with an eye toward digging across it. And a century later, the French Emperor Louis Napoleon went so far as to obtain a concession from Nicaragua to have a route surveyed.

The discovery of gold in California in 1848 provided a compelling argument for a more tolerable route between the two oceans. Thousands suffered the four-day trek across the Panamanian isthmus to reach the promised riches in California. Even the most hardy complained of the scorching heat and unexpectedly severe rains, of slime-covered river waters and vermin-infested huts. As one traveler wrote after crossing Panama, "I have nothing to say for the other routes but do not take this one."

The first attempt to improve the conditions of the journey across the isthmus was the construction of a trans-Panamanian railroad in 1855. Financed by American capital, the railroad cut travel time to four hours. But more important, it weighted the scales inevitably in favor of building a canal through Panama rather than planning an alternative route through Nicaragua, as the railroad would greatly facilitate the transport of workers and supplies through the inhospitable terrain.

In spite of the obvious American interest in a canal at Panama, the original canal project was controlled by France. In 1875, a French company was formed to explore the Panamanian route and gain a concession, and in 1879, 135 delegates attended the International Scientific Congress in Paris, where they discussed the precise route and possible types of canal.

Count Ferdinand de Lesseps, the French engineer who had built the Suez Canal, favored a similar sea-level trench in Panama. His colleague, Adolphe de Lépinay, who had visited the isthmus,

Right, the Bay of Panama as it appeared soon after Vasco Núñez de Balboa discovered the Pacific Ocean in 1513. Six years later the town of Panama was founded. It soon became an important base for the conquistadors and the port from which Incan treasure was sent across the isthmus to Colón and thence to Spain.

The construction of the Gaillard Cut (left) depended upon the railroad to transport equipment and crews and to haul earth and rock from the site.

Below left, the French engineer de Lesseps, whose attempt to build the canal ended in disaster. Below center, the Panamanian diplomat Bunau-Varilla, who signed a treaty in 1903 with the American Secretary of State John Hay (below right) granting the United States exclusive rights in perpetuity to the strip of land flanking the canal.

maintained that such a canal would be extremely difficult and expensive to dig because of the small but untamable rivers and unstable geological strata in the area. De Lépinay suggested the use of a different route or a series of locks. But the Scientific Congress stood behind de Lesseps's sea-level canal. Among the few members opposed to the proposal was Gustave Eiffel.

De Lesseps's company was in trouble from the start. The project had relied on the cooperation of the railroad, but the railroad refused to charge anything less than the regular fare to transport crews and freight into the jungle: $10 per second-class trip. The French had little choice but to buy out the railroad, at the sum of $25 million. The purchase was financed through a monumental share-selling campaign. The immensely popular seventy-five-year-old de Lesseps took his young family on a publicity tour to Panama, and many small French investors, impressed by his courage and trusting his judgment, volunteered their money.

By 1887, however, it was clear that a sea-level canal could not be dug. In trying to cut through the hill of Culebra, workers had discovered a series of geological strata that continually caved in, making excava-

tion impossible. De Lépinay's gloomy predictions were proved accurate. De Lesseps was therefore forced to revise the plans in favor of a system of ten sets of locks, to be designed, constructed, and installed by Gustave Eiffel.

But other adversities persisted. Within a few years over 20,000 workers had died of malaria and yellow fever. In December 1888, de Lesseps's company was declared bankrupt. An investigation of its affairs revealed an appalling story of bribery, corruption, and ineptitude (including the purchase of snow plows for the railroad). During the eight and a half years of construction, $262 million had been spent— but less than one-third had actually financed the canal. Criminal charges were brought against de Lesseps and his colleagues, and some of France's leading citizens were fined or jailed. Less than one-

quarter of the canal had been dug. In the wake of the disasters, the United States renewed its interest in the project, and in 1897, a Canal Commission was appointed by Congress. The commission initially recommended adoption of the Nicaraguan route which, though longer, would prove less expensive than paying what the French wanted for their rights in Panama. Eventually, the French lowered their price from $109 million to $40 million and the Panamanian route was chosen.

In 1903, the United States desire for permanent control of the proposed canal brought about the birth of the Republic of Panama. Under the Hay Herran Treaty, Colombia was to give the United States a strip of land across the isthmus, in return for an initial $10 million and $250,000 per year thereafter. But the Colombian senate refused to ratify the treaty. Encouraged by the United States, Panamanian proponents of the canal, who feared the loss of revenues from the waterway, rose in revolt against the government.

On November 3, 1903, Panama declared itself independent of Colombia, and the presence of an American warship, the U.S.S. *Nashville,* in the harbor of Colón prevented Colombian troops from quelling the insurrection. The new republic was recognized three days later by the United States and almost immediately by France, which was concerned with selling the canal rights. In return for the same terms earlier offered to Colombia, Panama granted the United States exclusive control of the canal zone in perpetuity, along with other sites for defense. However, the independence of Panama was not finally settled until 1921, when the United States paid Colombia $25 million in compensation for its loss of territory.

President Theodore Roosevelt eventually appointed as chief engineer John Stevens, a man of exceptional ability and stamina. Stevens had worked extensively in the Rocky Mountains and the western states and was familiar with the techniques and problems of open-pit mining. He had never previously been to Panama and arrived to find that the American project had degenerated into even more of a shambles than the French one.

Stevens, working between twelve and eighteen hours a day, inspired new spirit into the undertaking. He completely revised the priorities of the project, ordering a halt to all excavation. Panama City and Colón were to be sanitized and modernized, and new communities, piers, warehouses, and machine shops were to be built before the work continued.

Stevens convinced Congress that a system of locks, though difficult to build and to protect from sabotage, was preferable to a sea-level trench. He then resigned, for "purely personal" reasons.

The construction of the canal was completed under his replacement, Lieutenant Colonel G. W. Goethals, an outstanding military engineer. The enormous operation—the coordination of drilling, blasting, shoveling, and dirt hauling—required la-

Photographs taken during construction in the early 1900s (right) show the scale of the excavations. Much of the material removed from the site—a quarter of a billion cubic yards, or enough to build seventy Great Pyramids— was used to erect breakwaters and the Gatun Dam.

Below, two of the engineers who helped develop the canal's complex system of locks and channels. Chief engineer John Stevens was firmly opposed to a sea-level canal.

borers to remove a quarter of a billion cubic yards of earth in the process of constructing the largest locks in the world. Laboring in the tropical heat was backbreaking; countless workers died from grueling conditions and disease. But on August 15, 1914, the canal was finally opened to shipping.

The Panama Canal enables an average of thirty-eight vessels per day to avoid the eight-thousand-mile trip around Cape Horn. It begins on the Atlantic side with a

passage through Limón Bay, which is flanked by the twin cities of Cristóbal and Colón. A seven-mile-long channel leads from the breakwater to the Gatun Locks. In these three massive concrete chambers ships are lifted eighty-five feet to the level of Gatun Lake.

This lake, formed by damming the waters of the unruly Chagres River, solved both constructional and operational problems. Its creation eliminated the need to dig through a long expanse of terrain and,

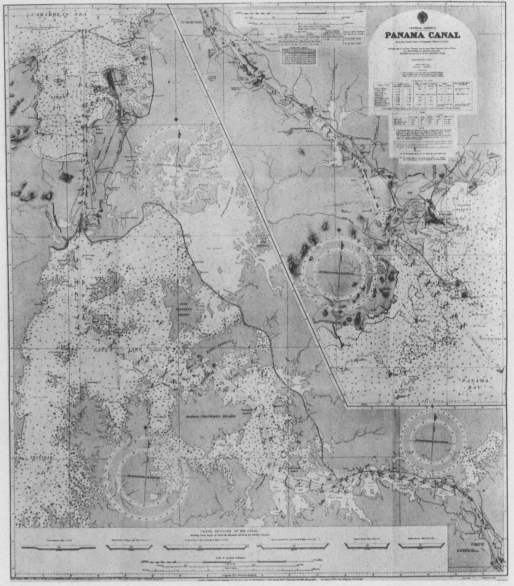

Left, a map of the Panama Canal showing its northwest (Caribbean) to southeast (Pacific) orientation.

Below left, the Cristóbal, *a ship belonging to the railroad company, making a trial run. The canal was unofficially opened to commercial navigation on August 15, 1914, although it was not formally inaugurated until World War I was over.*

moreover, provided a reserve of water for the operation of the locks.

A ship crosses the lake, which is 24 miles in length and 163 square miles in area, and then proceeds through the Gaillard Cut. This sheer gorge runs eight miles through the hill of Culebra—the same mountain that defeated the French. It is kept clear by constant dredging that removes as much as one million cubic yards of earth each year. At the end of the cut, the Pedro Miguel Locks lower the ship thirty-one feet to Miraflores Lake. From there, the ship is lowered again by the dual-chambered Miraflores Locks to the level of the Pacific, which varies as much as twelve feet depending upon the tide. It then travels through an eight-mile channel into the Bay of Panama.

The controversy surrounding the Panama Canal did not end when construction was completed. Its strategic value and vulnerability to sabotage and attack have made it a crucial American possession. But over the last two decades Panamanian agitation for greater control of the canal has resulted in a treaty by which the canal is to be turned over to Panama in the year 2000. The United States, however, will be accorded special rights of defense.

Today the political importance of the canal tends to overshadow its value as an extraordinary feat of engineering and ingenuity. Though the price was high, the Panama Canal is a rare success story. Not only did it open six months ahead of schedule, but the project was spared the corrupt practices—payroll padding, graft, and embezzlement—that so often characterize undertakings of such magnitude. But above all, the canal is a technical masterpiece—the realization of a 400-year-old dream.

Lever House

New York City

The bold originality and outstanding success of *Lever House* (1952) set the style for contemporary corporate architecture. Imitated everywhere, its decisive break with the past changed the face of the urban landscape. Lever House was the first skyscraper in New York to use a sheer glass-curtain façade (left). Perhaps most radical was the bold juxtaposition of the narrow vertical tower (nineteen stories high) upon a broad horizontal base. In contrast to the more typical ziggurat-shaped New York skyscrapers, Lever House did not make use of all the available space permitted under city regulations—an unprecedented victory of style over profitability. Because the building would be centrally air-conditioned (another novelty at the time), its architects chose not to interrupt the façade with operable windows. Consequently, an electrically operated gondola (right) had to be designed to be used when cleaning the exterior. This apparatus, now commonplace, attracted enormous curiosity when it was first introduced.

Preceding page, Lever House seen from the plaza of its equally famous successor, Mies van der Rohe's Seagram Building. In 1952, the precise forms, perpendicular tower, and glass sheathing of Lever House stood in dramatic contrast to the staid masonry façades of the surrounding buildings on Park Avenue.

Most of the offices in Lever House are situated in a narrow tower occupying only twenty-five percent of the building site. In a radical departure from tradition, the ground floor was replaced with an open-air garden plaza (above left and top right)—an idea since adopted by many other prestigious corporate buildings. A glass-enclosed area for special exhibits (bottom right) adjoins the courtyard. From the roof of the first floor (left and far left), another garden—reached from the employees' dining room (center right)—looks down into the courtyard.

Following page, the glass-curtain wall of the tower which so amazed the public only twenty-five years ago.

The interior of Lever House was executed by the industrial designer Raymond Loewy after extensive studies to determine the most comfortable and efficient environment.

The dark cubbyholes of previous commercial buildings were replaced by a free use of open spaces illuminated by fluorescent lighting (above left). Because the office tower is only sixty feet wide, no desk is more than twenty-five feet from a window.

Below left, above, and above right, a carpeted executive office, meeting room, and reception area on the twenty-first floor. Right, a typical corner office with a view down Park Avenue. Below, the data-processing center.

Lever House New York City

When the 1,200 New York employees of Lever Brothers moved into their new headquarters in 1952, they were immediately struck by an unexpected inconvenience: Lever House—a marvel of contemporary design—was afflicted by an elevator shortage. In designing the building, the architectural firm of Skidmore, Owings and Merrill had not planned for the rush of sightseers who thronged the building. "People acted as if this were the eighth wonder of the world," noted Lewis Mumford, one of the country's most highly regarded—and sternest—critics of architecture. "In many respects," he added, "this popular judgment is justified."

Less than thirty years have passed since Lever House opened its doors, but its revolutionary design was so successful that similar prismatic crystal towers now dominate the business districts of every large American city. Its practical floor plans, stainless-steel and glass-curtain walls, underground parking facilities, and elegantly utilitarian style are now taken for granted. Other aspects of the building are still con-

sidered novel, such as the sheltered, open-air plaza with a garden and the bold positioning of a narrow vertical tower over a broad horizontal base.

The design that the partners of Skidmore, Owings and Merrill proposed for the new building went far beyond the ordinary—but Lever Brothers was no ordinary corporate client. The enormous Dutch- and British-controlled multinational conglomerate had its fingers in many markets, including soap, margarine, and cosmetics. In the words of Nathaniel Owings, a founding partner of Skidmore, Owings and Merrill, it "had a quiet stranglehold on practically everything that bubbled, foamed or floated."

Although it has always been traditional for mammoth companies with vast holdings to proclaim their corporate images with equally large skyscrapers, Lever Brothers did not wish to call attention to its size in this way. What the corporation wanted was a smaller building that would

be distinctive for its "efficiency" and "everlasting cleanliness."

SOM won the commission for the building partly by chance. A few years before, on New Year's Eve, Owings was drinking with an old friend, a business consultant named George Fry. Owings, a short, chunky man with bright eyes (a writer for *Fortune* once said he bore a remarkable resemblance to Smokey the Bear) was fond of dice games, and he and Fry spent most of the evening shooting craps. "After a long run on the dice," Owings recalled later, "I seemed to have all George's money." Owings, whose talents were legendary for manipulating other people in behalf of what he considered their mutual interest, decided to give Fry back all his money. Fry showed his gratitude by advancing a highly confidential business tip: Lever Brothers was about to build a new headquarters in New York and was looking for an architect. Owings quickly passed this news on to his asso-

The architect's sketch (below) and model (right) illustrate the basic design of Lever House: an open plaza at pavement level, a wide first floor supported on columns, and, above, a narrow vertical office tower—whose unorthodox shape was initially likened to an office filing cabinet.

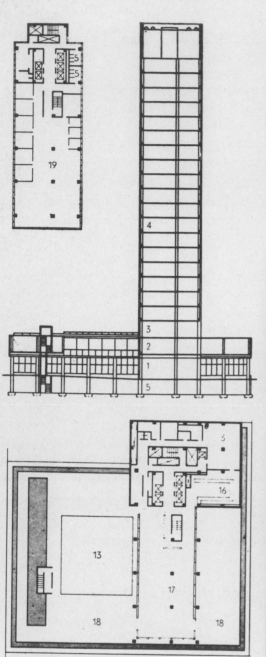

Above, drawings of Lever House by Skidmore, Owings and Merrill, showing, in ascending order, the roof plan of the horizontal block from which the narrower tower rises, a cross section of the building, and a standard layout of one of the floors in the tower.

Above right, SOM's Union Carbide Building (1960), which has also become a Park Avenue landmark.

ciate Louis Skidmore, and within two weeks the partners had signed a contract.

The partnership of Skidmore and Owings had begun after the two young architects had worked together on the 1933–1934 "Century of Progress" exposi-tion. Because of the Depression, most of the original plans for the fair were aban-doned, and in the ensuing confusion Skid-more—a slender, soft-spoken man with a waxed mustache who characteristically wore a raccoon coat—persuaded the fair's directors to appoint him chief designer. He in turn took on Owings, whose sister he had recently married, as development su-pervisor. "Skid and I took the fair over," Owings recalled afterward. "We had to devise solutions, do a bare minimum, use the simplest materials—we built the pavil-ions out of beaverboard." More than seven hundred companies had exhibits at the fair, and the two young men gained invaluable selling and logistical experi-ence in their dealings with corporate exec-utives. One of these was H. J. Heinz, who informed Skidmore that his company's exhibit would be a giant 300-foot papier-mâché pickle. Skidmore, who thought the idea vulgar, refused to grant permission for the exhibit and proposed instead a Heinz exhibit of historical kitchens, filled with Heinz products. Heinz had to agree that the idea was intriguing—and an unu-sually practical one, too, considering that it had come from an architect.

A year after the fair closed, the paths of Owings and Skidmore crossed again at London's Paddington Station, where they sat down on a pair of steamer trunks and decided to become partners. At that time even more than now, most architectural offices consisted of a single chief designer surrounded by assistants. But after working together at the fair, Skidmore and Owings had learned the value of a team approach. Owings's forte was dreaming up grandiose projects and persuading clients to agree to them. "I launched big ideas," he said, "because they were more easily launched than small ones." Skidmore's role in the partnership would be to see to the architectural details once the projects were under way. As they planned it, their new firm would be a corporate umbrella under which many designers would work. "We decided that the young designer would be free to try anything," Owings explained later. "We would guide him, but we would not inhibit him." Owings's reference to freedom had one important proviso—it was a freedom to try anything modern.

In 1936, the two opened their first office—a small attic in a building overlooking Chicago's Michigan Avenue. They could not afford the rent of $50 a month, so they arranged to remodel the other offices in the building in lieu of payment. A short time later, Skidmore opened a second small office in New York. Eventually, the company would have separate offices in many cities, each independent but able to call on the others for assistance on large projects.

In 1939, the firm expanded its expertise by taking on the structural engineer John Merrill and, soon thereafter, added other partners with diverse specialties. Thus, when war curtailed most private building, SOM had the resources to take on large projects for the government, one of which *Architectural Forum* called "the best job of emergency planning to come out of the war." By 1945, the young office had grown to 450 employees and had assumed the organizational structure that would make it so appealing. As one observer commented, "Since the firm understands corporate structure and has an appreciation of the hierarchy of specialized responsibility, it has a natural acceptance with corporate clients."

One of SOM's young New York part-

ners was Gordon Bunshaft, a headstrong and self-confident graduate of MIT. Although Owings considered him a "temperamental artist," Bunshaft flourished at SOM. As he put it, "The others take care of the headaches, and I am in charge of the design." Bunshaft was responsible for SOM's commercially successful and uniquely American stylistic formula: a synthesis of the rationality of the late nineteenth-century Chicago School—with its emphasis on simplicity, efficiency, and high technology—and the Abstract Expressionist's enthusiasm for the "glass ar-

Above, the Lower Manhattan skyline dominated by SOM's Chase Manhattan Bank Building (1961). Unlike Lever House, this sixty-story tower, which houses more than 15,000 employees, does not attempt to maintain the line of its adjacent street but rather rises abruptly from a large open plaza.

Below left, an "exploded" partial perspective showing in horizontal cross section the sidewalk level of Lever House.

Below, SOM's Inland Steel Building (1958), which Mies van der Rohe once called "the best building in Chicago."

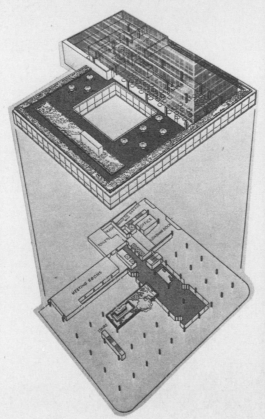

chitecture" of such European modernists as Walter Gropius and Mies van der Rohe. It was Bunshaft who would design Lever House.

One request made by Lever Brothers was for a building where not just the windows but "every inch of the exterior surface" could be "washed regularly." Bunshaft was happy to comply and suggested that the entire external skin of the building be sheathed in dazzling blue-green, tinted glass panels set in a grid of stainless-steel glazing bars. Although the glass would appear colorless from inside the building, it would nevertheless absorb thirty-five percent of the sun's heat. Seen from the street, the glazed walls would reflect the sky and neighboring buildings.

SOM's proposal for the new building's ground floor was also extraordinary: There was to be no ground floor—the space would be used instead for an open-air garden plaza. For this Lever Brothers had to forego $250,000 a year in rentals

from shops. The only enclosed space at the pavement level would be a glass-walled exhibition gallery, a small auditorium, and an experimental kitchen where, as one Lever employee put it, the company could demonstrate "the strength of Breeze, the purity of Spry."

Above the plaza, on stilts, would stand the first real floor, which was designed to house a large office area covering most of the building site. Its roof, in turn, would be a private garden, connected to the company cafeteria, for Lever employees. The remaining eighteen floors would consist of a narrow tower less than sixty feet wide, occupying only twenty-five percent of the total building site and leaving the rest of the potential building space unused. Because of the tower's narrowness, the interior would receive excellent light, and no desk would be more than twenty-five feet from a window. Furthermore, the positioning of this vertical tower above the wide horizontal slab of the first floor and

plaza—perhaps not accidentally, a huge backward "L"—would become a readily identifiable corporate symbol for Lever.

The opening of Lever House assured SOM's future dominance in American business architecture. Ahead lay such accomplishments as the Inland Steel Building, which Mies van der Rohe once called "the best building in Chicago," the Chase Manhattan Building, the Union Carbide Building, and the Air Force Academy at Colorado Springs. By the late 1950s, SOM had changed the face of corporate America, and no other design firm could hope to match the number of commissions and distinguished awards it received. Lever House also indirectly benefited other architectural firms; when dealing with balking clients, they could cite it as an example of a contemporary design that worked. In fact, many observers think Lever House worked so well that, despite the thousands of imitations, its overall excellence remains unsurpassed.

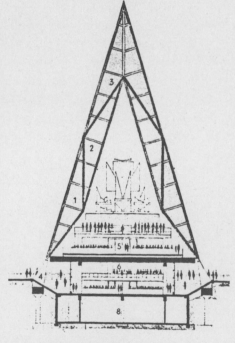

SOM also designed the U.S. Air Force Academy at Colorado Springs (1962). The firm's proposal for the academy's chapel (model, left and above, cross section), with its seventeen-spire, accordion-shaped roof, was eventually built despite intense military and Congressional opposition.

Hoover Dam

Arizona/Nevada

Hoover Dam fits like a stopper into a particularly narrow neck of the deeply cut Black Canyon. The dam, built between 1931 and 1936, is named after President Herbert Hoover. Lake Mead, the artificial lake created by the dam, holds 30,500,000 acre-feet of water (one acre, one foot deep). This volume is the approximate equivalent of two years' flow of the Colorado River. A road across the 1,244-foot-long top of the dam links Arizona on the right with Nevada on the left. Above the dam on either side of the lake are emergency spillways, for use should there be a flood at a time when the lake is already filled.

Top left, twin pairs of water intake towers joined together and to the dam by concrete bridges. The towers, some 395 feet in height, regulate the flow of water from Lake Mead. They feed into pipes that skirt the dam, passing under the rocky shoulders of the Black Canyon.

Center and bottom left, the Colorado River channel at the foot of the dam between the wings of the electricity generating plant. As a young, fast-flowing river that descends in abrupt drops from high mountains to sea level, the Colorado is particularly suited to the production of hydroelectric power. The plant added some ten percent to the horsepower available in 1936 for generating electricity in the United States.

Above right, the dam seen from above Lake Mead. The 115-mile-long lake provides fishing and boating facilities in this desert region. At the left of the photo is the Arizona spillway.

Below right, the dam and the electricity generating plant. Only the cars on the roadway are reminders of the immense scale of the dam, which is 726 feet high.

Left, one of the two Nevada intake towers. Its clean, angular design is reminiscent of much Art Deco American skyscraper construction in the 1930s. The part above water is about one-sixth of its total height.

The lean, strictly functional design of the dam's outlying sections (above) harmonizes well with the massive natural backdrop. Above right, the wings of the power plant, seen from the crest of the dam. Below, the Arizona spillway. During flood conditions, water can be discharged through each spillway at the speed of almost 120 miles per hour.

The thirty-foot-high, winged figures by Oscar Hansen (above), sculpted in bronze on bases of polished black granite, stand near one end of the dam. From other perspectives, the contrasting textures of water, rock, and metal artistically complement the unembellished surfaces of the dam.

Top left, above, and above right, the control room of the electricity generating station. From here, electricity is distributed across a radius of some 300 miles, including all of Arizona and southern California. Los Angeles was the first city to tap the dam's supply of electricity, which is sent there by a 260-mile transmission system built by the city itself. Center left, a generator room in the Nevada wing of the power plant.

Left and right, the rich agricultural lands of the Imperial Valley, whose irrigation canals and ditches are filled exclusively by Colorado River water. Water from Lake Mead can irrigate about one million acres of farm land in California, Arizona, and Nevada.

Following page, pylons, planted deeply in the rocky cliff top, radiating outward from the electricity generating plant.

Hoover Dam Arizona/Nevada

The systematic attempt to tame and transform nature is a recurrent theme in recent world history. The Industrial Revolution provided the tools, and a growing population created the necessity. Hot on the heels of visionaries and adventurers in search of exploitable sources of natural wealth came efficient armies sponsored by government sources and entrepreneurs alike: surveyors, agronomists, geologists, and, of course, engineers. From the mid-nineteenth century onward, such glamorous projects as the Suez and Panama canals, the Union Pacific and Trans-Siberian railroads, and tunnels through the Alps all caught and fed the public imagination. Meanwhile, the drive to modernize agriculture and break the isolation of hitherto backward sections of the country continued. Electrification, flood control, and the reclamation of once-useless land became the order of the day.

The Boulder Canyon Project, built from 1931 to 1936 along the Colorado River in the Southwest, was the first of many major projects that transformed rural America. Talk of harnessing the river had begun seriously in the 1900s, spurred on by plans to transform the arid Imperial Valley of southern California into a year-round agricultural hothouse. It was believed that through irrigation this rich but arid soil would become fertile. However, the proposal provoked intense controversy among the southwestern states over how to share the water—the key to growth and prosperity in that area of the country.

In the 1920s, after many complicated negotiations that involved the southwestern states and the federal government, an agreement was finally reached. The U.S. Bureau of Reclamation then began to give serious thought to a complex project whose cornerstone was the Hoover Dam.

Political maneuvers played a decisive role in what turned out to be a complicated tug of war—naming the dam. Originally called the Boulder Dam, it was renamed for Herbert Hoover during his presidency. In 1933, under the Democrats, it became Boulder Dam again, but it was officially renamed Hoover Dam by a Republican-dominated Congress in 1947. Hoover it has since remained.

The purpose of the project was to harness and use the water of the vast Colorado River. From its source in northern Colorado, the river ran 1,500 miles to the Gulf of California, carving almost a thousand miles of canyons—the most spectacular of which is the Grand Canyon. After flowing through southeastern Utah and northwestern Arizona, the river serves as the boundary, first between Nevada and Arizona and then between California and Arizona. Because so much of the water has been diverted, the river now crosses the Mexican border and dies in the desert. In its passage, the river drains nearly 250,000 square miles, including virtually all of Arizona, much of Utah and Colorado, and parts of Wyoming, Nevada, New Mexico, and California.

Major obstacles had to be overcome before the Colorado could be used for irrigation and generating electric power. First, there was the extraordinary amount of silt that the river carried downstream to

Below left, President Herbert Hoover, whose experience as an engineer and in the Southwest helped strengthen the government's role in the complex—and controversial—political maneuvering that preceded the project.

Below, an aerial drawing showing Hoover Dam. The nearby Boulder City construction camp was tightly controlled by the federal government. The streets were laid out symmetrically and many of the Spanish colonial-style buildings were air conditioned.

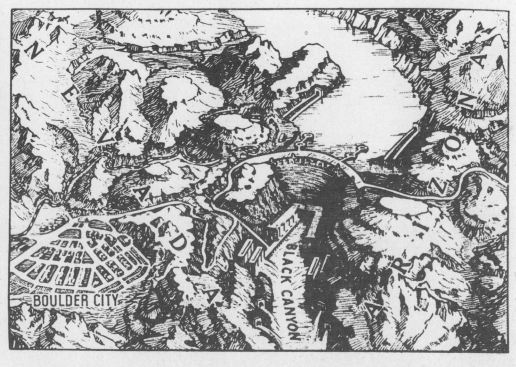

1929

BOULDER CITY

Right, a huge overhead crane transporting a twenty-ton bucket of wet concrete from the concrete plant, to be tipped into the wooden forms at the dam site. Between June 1933 and May 1935, 3,250,000 cubic yards of concrete were placed in the dam.

dump at random, much of it into the sea. Not only was valuable soil lost in this way, but the water also had to be filtered before it could be used in homes. The waters, it was said, were too thick to drink and too thin to plow. Farming costs were increased by the constant need to remove the silt that clogged the irrigation ditches. Silt also clogged the lower Colorado itself, heightening an already dangerous possibility of flooding.

The annual floods of late spring often had terrible force, as did the frequent flash floods that followed summer thunderstorms. Dams were smashed, farm land ruined, and lives lost. Imperial Valley was disastrously inundated several times in 1905 and 1906, despite the construction of expensive, and ever higher, levees. After the annual floods, the lower Colorado would withhold its waters from farm lands for three to seven months from August onward. Then melting snow in its upper basin—Utah, and particularly Wyoming and Colorado—would fill it anew. The river was both capricious and dangerous; Boulder Dam was meant to bring it to heel.

During its steep descent to the sea from the plateau of the upper basin—8,000 feet above sea level at its highest point—the Colorado had cut a narrow gorge, sometimes a mile deep, through the mountains. This provided a number of ready-made sites for a dam. Eventually the federal government decided on Black Canyon, situated on the Arizona-Nevada boundary some thirty miles southeast of Las Vegas. The immediate area was rugged and isolated but contained good gravel deposits, potential quarries, and enough level land for a construction camp.

The width of the canyon at the pro-

posed dam site was only 330 feet, while it was 900 feet deep at the dam's crest. This promised both considerable savings in materials and construction time and a high electricity generating capacity. The canyon itself was of volcanic rock, which was easily drilled, required few supports when tunneled, and would provide a firm foundation and side abutments for the dam.

Black Canyon had other advantages. A dam there would be below the river's major tributaries and so could control most floods and the torrents of silt. It was also near enough to the California and Arizona flat lands to handle their irrigation needs as well as to provide electric power for the cities of southern California.

An elaborate infrastructure had to be created before construction could begin on the dam itself, which would be the tallest on earth. In September 1930, work began on a railroad from the Union Pacific line at Las Vegas to the dam site. Vast amounts of equipment and supplies were brought in, including locomotives, gravel cars, cableways, housing, food, and medical supplies. The town of Boulder City was built on federal land and under federal control to house some 5,000 workers and their families. A successful effort was made to avoid the boom-town, honky-tonk atmosphere of most isolated construction camps.

Pragmatism as well as a respect for a regulated, wholesome environment were

Above, a laborer working on the steel reinforcement piers of the intake towers. Left, one of the intake towers, seen with its lower levels already cast in concrete.

Right, the dam as it neared completion. The cable car lines above the site saved invaluable time, labor, and cost in shunting material to and fro.

behind this conscious attempt to counter-act the independent, footloose tradition of construction work. There was no doubt that the undertaking was both demanding and dangerous—over a hundred workers were to die in the course of the project. There was bitter cold in winter and stifling heat in summer. For those working at the bottom of Black Canyon, where the heat was most intense, canteens of water and salt tablets were essential for survival. To escape the heat and meet deadlines, it was often necessary to work at night under floodlights.

Though they often seemed oppressive, the breakneck schedules meant greater profits for the contractors. Speed was of the essence for Six Companies of San

Francisco, the consortium of experienced western construction companies that won the contract in March 1931 for the electric power plant and much—though not all—of the dam work. Their bid was $49 million, a huge sum for those days. Other contracts brought the total cost of the dam to $120 million. One of the leaders of the Six Companies consortium was Henry J. Kaiser, who later helped build Grand Coulee Dam and mass-produced merchant ships on an assembly-line basis during World War II.

Construction began immediately. First, men on ropes and scaffolds descended from the canyon rim. Using jackhammers and dynamite, they then struck loose boulders from the sides in an effort to

avert accidents caused by falling debris. The second stage of the preparatory process involved the stream bed itself. A new route had to be created for the Colorado, leaving the riverbed open to the excavators, who would dig through 200 feet of sand to reach bedrock. Four, three-quarter-mile tunnels diverting the river around the dam site were drilled and dynamited during 1931–1932. They later formed an integral part of the dam system.

A cofferdam just above the dam site then forced the river into its new course, while another cofferdam farther down river prevented the water from backing up onto the construction site. There, earth-moving equipment and trucks removed the sand and prepared for the emplacement of wooden framework, steel bars, and—eventually—concrete.

The dam was to be of the arch-gravity type, a huge mass of concrete dependent on its arched form supported by the canyon walls, to resist the pressure of the water behind it. The dam is 660 feet thick at its base, but only 245 feet thick at the top. In cross section it is similar to a right triangle, with its vertical side facing upriver against the current, while a gently sloping reverse side broadens out as it nears the riverbed.

The dam has a total of four tunnels. One pair feeds water from Lake Mead, the 115-mile-long reservoir above the dam, into the powerhouse. The other two tunnels function as spillways in an emer-gency, accommodating any sudden surge of water that might otherwise sweep over the dam.

The water is controlled by four intake towers, each nearly 400 feet high, set on both sides of the dam in pairs. Below the dam is the powerhouse, which was the largest in the world when it was first built. This is a U-shaped structure, some twenty stories high, its wings resting on opposite river banks. The seventeen generators account for 1.8 million horsepower, produc-ing over four billion kilowatt-hours an-nually. This production has been vital for southern California in general, and for Los Angeles in particular. In the autumn of 1937, the city began receiving electricity over pylon and cable transmission lines.

After five years of work, the dam was completed in March 1936, more than two years ahead of schedule. There had been no labor problems. The engineers and ad-ministrators had been able to solve prob-lems as they occurred. And the pessimistic predictions of structural disasters had not materialized.

The stability and prosperity of southern California and western Arizona are due largely to the life-giving water and energy made possible by Hoover Dam. In fact, the roots of the recent economic growth of the entire Sun Belt of the United States can be traced, at least in part, to those early enthusiasts who were willing to take a risk and make what many considered a foolhardy attempt to master the Colorado.

Far left, teams of workers, called "high-scalers," stripping tons of loose, projecting rock from the walls of the canyon. They are suspended by steel cables.

Above, a cable car transporting workers to one of the many sites in the canyon inacces-sible to road or rail.

Near left, the great basin of the Nevada spillway. Its counter-part, the Arizona spill-way, also takes off ex-cess water during floods.

Graythorp I

North Sea

Preceding page, Graythorp I, looming over a sinister North Sea. This was the first oil-production platform erected in the Forties Field, midway between Norway and Scotland. Along with its three sister platforms, this technological monster produces a staggering 500,000 barrels of crude oil per day.

The 700-foot-high tower weighs 30,000 tons and represents an investment of $145 million. On June 29, 1974, the tower began its journey out to the oil field (these pages). The dry-dock basin was flooded (center near right), the gate removed (right), and the structure, towed by the two most powerful tugs in the world, began its 275-mile, three-day journey from the dock (immediately below) through the mouth of the River Tees (bottom) to its emplacement in 400 feet of water 100 miles northeast of Aberdeen (far right).

The weather was a crucial consideration during the emplacement. North Sea conditions are notorious: 273 days in any one year are often officially described as "bad" and thirty-nine as "marginal." The least inclement conditions, termed the "weather window," occur in late summer. Unexpected breaks in the weather window caused numerous delays and considerable anxiety to project managers and insurers. Continual reports were maintained from a satellite, three weather ships, and several other North Sea rigs as well as the London Weather Center. An unanticipated storm—all too common in this part of the world—could easily have reduced the ungainly floating tower to a mere "hazard to navigation."

Far left, the most critical moment of the emplacement of the tower. First, with the help of computers, the rear tanks of the flotation pontoons were flooded, tipping the structure to an angle of five degrees. Then came a crash dive from five to forty-five degrees (far left, first, second, and third photos) which took only thirty-four seconds—and required the precision of a moon shot. Gradual flooding of the remaining tanks submerged the structure to an angle of ninety degrees (far left bottom) before it was settled in its upright position on the sea bed (immediately above). With the tower in its final position and the pontoons removed, the gigantic crane barge Thor (top)—a former 50,000-ton tanker—drove in the piles that secure it to the sea floor.

After weather delays, which cost $240,000 a day in standby costs, the first modular section of the platform was lifted onto Graythorp I in October 1974 (left). The problem of mounting these modules has been compared to lifting several 2,000-ton slices of cake and sliding them into a three-tiered cake rack. The lift required two hours, and a sudden squall might have set the sections swinging in a wild arc around the crane operator.

The first platforms in the North Sea, including Graythorp I, were designed and managed by the Houston-based firm of Brown and Root. Large-scale offshore drilling had begun in 1946 off Texas and Louisiana, establishing American predominance in offshore technology. But the technological scale of Gulf of Mexico structures, set in 60 to 100 feet of water, seems almost insignificant compared to the task of installing a rig in 400 feet of water in the middle of the savage North Sea. Now, due to shrinking oil reserves in an energy-starved world, there are plans to drill in 2,000 feet of water—a feat which will require an even greater amount of technical sophistication.

Clockwise, from near right: the crane barge Hercules makes ready to remove the pontoon; Thor prepares to drive one of the piles attached to the tubular legs of the tower; the control cabin of the control ship OIL Producer monitors the emplacement of the tower; technicians on the pontoon (bottom right and below) give some sense of its true size; and the crane operator's cab on Thor (left).

The modular design of Graythorp I *allowed much of the work to be executed onshore and insured that installation could be as rapid as possible. Production and drilling equipment are contained within the three-tiered sets of modules. The top level is occupied mainly by the central drilling derrick, storage, and generators while a helicopter deck and the flare stack hang precipitously off the side. The energy—gas—required by the platform is drawn directly from the oil and gas mixture pumped up from the field below. The bottom two levels of modules house production items and four stories of accommodations for workers. Supply ships (below and right) and helicopters (left) are a regular link between this artificial island and the mainland.*

Following page, a triumphant Graythorp I, *now fully operational. The men just visible on the platforms give some idea of the mammoth scale of the rig.*

Graythorp I
North Sea

Architecture, as art, could not have been further from the minds of those responsible for building *Graythorp I,* the first oil-production platform in the North Sea. Their concerns were both practical and immediate: the efficient extraction of millions of tons of crude oil from 8,000 feet below the floor of the North Sea and its transportation via submarine and underground pipeline to a refinery some 250 miles distant.

Yet *Graythorp* can also be viewed as an architectural monument in an age where the relationship of architecture and engineering is complex and their provinces are blurred. In its exploration of the limits of technology, *Graythorp* is one of the supreme triumphs of our century. And in its unadorned use of metal, its sheer absence of style, it ranks among other purely functional structures of the twentieth century—grain elevators, silos, factories, furnaces, bridges, and derricks—which have earned themselves the appellation "architectural" engineering. Their rigorously honest forms have radically altered the modern landscape—and seascape—in an unprecedented way.

Graythorp has since been joined by three platforms, each about three miles apart, designed to tap the resources of the Forties Field over the next twenty to thirty years. Together they form a small archi-

pelago of islands, each constructed of prefabricated modules fitted into a gigantic steel tower which is largely submerged beneath the turbulent sea.

The exploitation of oil and natural gas below the sea bed is a relatively new science fostered by an urgent need to discover new energy reserves. The era of offshore oil prospecting opened soon after World War II, with large-scale drilling off the coast of Texas and Louisiana. The experience gained from these early opera-

tions in the Gulf of Mexico established American predominance in offshore technology. In Europe, where there had never seemed to be much oil, such exploration was slower to get under way. But in 1959, a vast onshore deposit of natural gas was discovered at Groningen on the coast of Holland. This exciting discovery led geologists to expect that there might be comparable deposits under the neighboring North Sea.

At various times in the past, the area

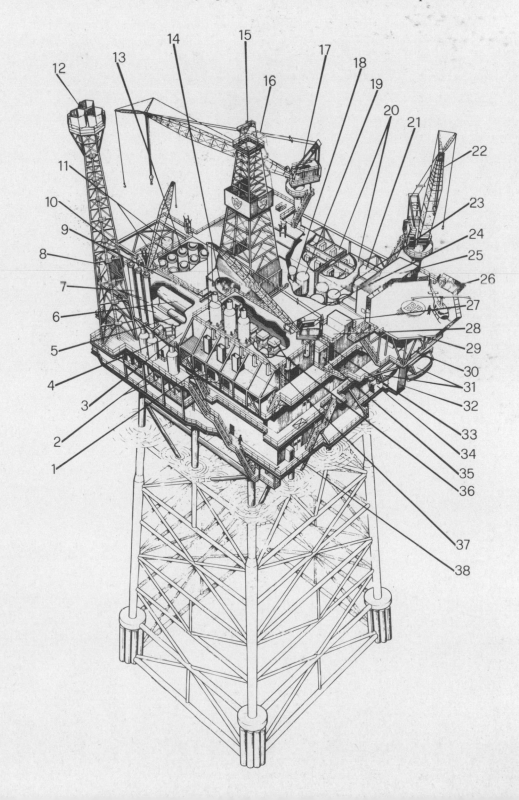

Right, partial cutaway drawings of Graythorp I *in the North Sea, illustrating its efficient organization. It consists of a tower supporting three layers, each 170 feet square, of modular accommodation units all placed in position at the offshore site.*

now covered by the North Sea has been land, joining Continental Europe and the British Isles. For extended periods of history, however, it has been a sea, and sediments have been deposited from the surrounding lands. It is in such sediments, some of which are 20,000 feet thick, that oil and gas occur.

Although the geological indications were favorable, crews exploring for oil in the North Sea had to confront probably the world's worst offshore weather conditions. For about two-thirds of the winter, wind speed is above seventeen knots and exceeds twenty-eight knots during much of the season. Gusts of over 100 knots and 60-foot waves are common. Extreme storm conditions of 140-knot winds and 100-foot waves are statistically probable "once every hundred years," although Forties hands say that "once every hundred years" comes perilously close each year. Air temperatures are below freezing for long periods; fog and rain often reduce visibility to near zero. To make matters worse, the weather conditions are extremely variable and difficult to predict.

In October 1970, British Petroleum discovered Britain's first major oil deposit, the Forties Field, 110 miles northeast of Aberdeen. The next step was to develop a production capability. Previous methods of production were simply inadequate to the task of erecting platforms in the hostile North Sea. Engineers had never had to deal with such extreme weather conditions. The bearing capacity of the underlying rock structure and the strong tidal currents were also unknowns. Yet the Houston-based firm of Brown and Root not only developed production rigs to operate in these difficult conditions, but they also succeeded in designing, fabricating, and installing them in a remarkably short time. In November 1975, just five years after the initial strike in the Forties Field, the first oil was pumped ashore.

To call *Graythorp I* a platform is misleading. It is, in effect, a tall steel tower, standing on the ocean floor, held by piles driven hundreds of feet into the bedrock. The tubular, space frame structure supports a working surface of equipment and accommodation modules arranged in three decks each 170 feet square. There is also, of course, a drilling rig and a helicopter landing pad as well as living space for ninety-six men.

The 700-foot-high platform stands in 400 feet of water. Its function is to drill more than twenty widely dispersed wells from this fixed location to the oil-bearing strata 7,000 feet below the sea bed. When fully operational, *Graythorp I* will have a production capacity of 125,000 barrels per day and an anticipated lifespan of twenty to thirty years.

The construction of *Graythorp* presented its own problems. For one thing, the platform was still being designed as it was being built. And, of course, a platform of its size had never been attempted before. When completed, it would contain more metal than was used in the enor-

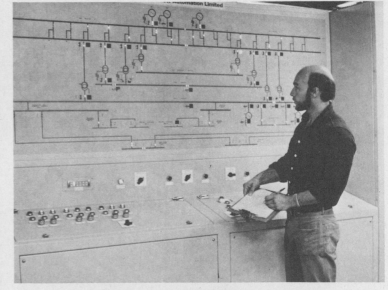

Drilling installations are the nucleus of the platform. A large panel in the control room (above) registers data coming from the wellheads (far left and near left), which are operational twenty-four hours a day.

mous nineteenth-century Forth Railway Bridge and four times the amount used in the Eiffel Tower. In fact, it would be almost large enough to encapsulate the Houses of Parliament, including Big Ben. Because of its unwieldiness, the tower itself was to be built on its side in a dry dock, and the modular accommodations and equipment units were then to be hoisted into position at sea.

To begin with, the construction facilities themselves had to be built. What was required for a dry dock was a flat area adjacent to deep water. After much research, a disused ship repair yard at Graythorp on Teesside was chosen. Once the site was opened, 700 local laborers lined up at the gates in the hope of landing a job. But the construction standards were so high that even trained shipyard workers were given a familiarization course. The vast dry dock—in which the tower would be built on top of a pontoon—took months to construct. When the dry dock was flooded on completion, the whole construction floated free in the water and was pulled out to sea by a team of tugs.

One of the problems the platform builders had to face was the apparently simple one—lifting things. The largest existing land cranes were able to lift a mere 800 tons, so that a complex orchestration of seven cranes was needed to lift assembled portions of the tower into position. Since this operation was not possible at sea, the engineers boldly designed a crane barge—in fact, a converted 50,000-ton oil tanker—that could lift loads of between 1,600 and 2,000 tons. This crane, the largest in the world, was used in the emplacement of the platforms.

The thirty-two-inch diameter of the underwater pipeline was also a record breaker: Nothing of its size had ever been laid underwater before. The crude oil produced by *Graythorp* is pumped through this pipeline 110 miles to Cruden Bay on the coast of Scotland. From there it goes by an underground pipeline an additional 135 miles to an oil refinery at Grange-mouth on the Firth of Forth.

To finance the enterprise, British Petroleum negotiated the largest private financing ever arranged, a loan of £370 million, from a syndicate of no less than sixty-six banks in twelve countries. The eventual cost of Forties development is estimated at £750 million. On the occasion of the launching of the second platform to be emplaced in this field, one of the Lloyds brokers who had insured the floating platforms for £50 million commented that it was "the largest sum that's ever been on the end of a piece of string."

The production of domestic oil has provided a major boost to the flagging British economy. Before the discovery of North Sea oil, Britain was obliged to import all its oil and its economy was based on coal. It now produces fifty percent of its needs and is expected to be self-sufficient by 1980. Britain is well aware of the supreme importance of this energy reserve. On November 3, 1975, Queen Elizabeth herself

Up to ninety-six men live and work at the platform, which is equipped with (clockwise from below left): kitchen, laundry, canteen, and a cabin containing desks, chairs, and radios.

Right, the arrival of the helicopter bringing newspapers, mail, and films to men on the platform.

pushed a button to inaugurate the flow of North Sea oil into the pipeline. Afterward Prime Minister Harold Wilson predicted that "a new industrial revolution" was in store for Britain.

For the moment, man has triumphed over nature. But these heroic examples of advanced engineering are an urgent response to the dwindling energy resources upon which our world economy is based. Unlike say, Stonehenge, which wears an aspect of eternity, the North Sea platforms were designed and built to last only twenty to thirty years, after which time they will probably be dismantled.

In our own decade, architects and engineers have begun to turn their thinking toward soft-technology solutions, such as solar and wind energy. Meanwhile, the four platforms of the Forties Field continue to pump their 500,000 barrels a day homeward to feed the sagging post-colonial British economy and prepare it for the advent of the ultimate oil crisis—the day when oil cannot be had at any price.

This peculiar situation makes *Graythorp I* an intriguing monument, for it was constructed under conditions of the greatest duress, and with the obsolescence of its own function clearly in mind. It is a monument not to the glory of its age but to its imminent death—a kind of stopgap monument to the new age which none of us can yet foresee.

Above left, an artist's rendering of a North Sea platform showing the tower set on the sea bed and modules above sea level.

Above, a model of Highland I, *one of* Graythorp I's *sister platforms in the Forties Field.*

Charles De Gaulle Airport

Roissy-en-France

Fifteen miles northeast of Paris at Roissy lies the starkly modern Charles De Gaulle Airport (preceding page). The nucleus of the airport is the main terminal building, which contains the principal passenger and baggage-handling facilities. Its circular shape (center left and bottom row) is a function of the access roads which dip under a taxi way, divide into ramps, and sweep around the building at the departure and arrival levels.

Surrounding the main terminal building are seven satellite terminals, from which passengers disembark and board their planes. When the construction is finished, Charles De Gaulle will be able to accommodate over thirty million people each year. Top left, a Concorde at rest between two of the satellite terminals. Above right, the airport hotel.

What may look like a set for a science-fiction movie is actually the central atrium of the terminal. Mobile floor strips, called travelators, carry passengers through glass tubes to the various parts of the building. The apparently helter-skelter arrangement of the tubes is deceptive. Basically, there are three pairs of tubes originating at points ninety degrees from each other on the mezzanine level. One tube of each pair transports passengers up from the departure level; the other takes arriving passengers up to the customs level. The otherwise inaccessible glass tubes are washed by a rotating, three-legged window-washer crane (above right).

The interior of Charles De Gaulle Airport is as functional as its exterior. Top right, the main entrance to the circular terminal on the same level as the entrance roadway. Above left, the departure (ticketing) level of the terminal. The sweep of the building can be felt as it curves around out of sight. Below far left, the terminal crowded with passengers waiting to depart. The serpentine seating plan (near left, center and bottom) adds a touch of color to the otherwise uniformly gray complex. Center right, the computerized luggage-handling system, one of the major innovations at the airport. Passengers with time on their hands may browse in the many duty-free shops and fancy boutiques (bottom right) also found in the terminal.

The section of Charles De Gaulle Airport currently operating was completed in March 1974 and handles between six and eight million travelers each year. The nerve center of the complex is the 250-foot central control tower (left), the tallest structure at Charles De Gaulle.

Above right, one of the satellite terminals seen from the main building. The Concorde in the background adds to the futuristic ambiance of the airport. Below right, another Concorde attached to an extensible gangway leading to a satellite terminal. These gangways (below) can be extended to 150 feet.

Charles De Gaulle Airport Roissy-en-France

In 1969, construction began on a major international airport at the village of Roissy, now renamed Roissy-en-France, fifteen miles northeast of Paris. The site of this exotic, attention-getting airport covers an area one-third the size of Paris. The first stage of construction, which took five years, cost a staggering $330 million. Several years later, the airport is still not finished, though millions of passengers have already passed through the completed terminal building known as Aérogare No. 1—true to the noticeably futuristic spirit of the airport.

A project of such awesome scale naturally demanded a suitably prestigious name. Thus, the airport at Roissy was dedicated to France's last great son of the nineteenth century, General Charles De Gaulle, who headed the government during World War II and was later elected president.

There is a touch of irony in the name. Charles De Gaulle was the quintessence of France. And he had an aristocratic contempt for the parvenu pretensions—to political influence and prestige and technological genius—of the New World. It wasn't that he hated America; he merely pitied it for not being France. Yet from the air, Charles De Gaulle Airport resembles strongly the idea (which often differs from the reality) of a large American airport. One expects to see Los Angeles or Houston over the horizon, not Paris.

For "Roissy," as the French simplify it, was born out of a single grand but simple gesture. It consists of a circular "bagel-shaped" building at its center (the terminal and parking garage) with seven smaller structures (the aircraft loading gates) set like satellites around it. This particular scheme was first used decades ago in Los Angeles. The use of such an almost simplistic design concept characterizes a great deal of modern American building.

On the other hand, each detail of the airport's plan is so logical and rational that it can also be viewed as typically French. In ambiance, however, it is in a class of its own. Roissy has neither the Coney Island feeling of New York's La Guardia nor the historical atmosphere of Orly, also near Paris, where Lindbergh ended his famous flight in 1927. It seems instead to belong in the twenty-first century.

The French rationality underlying the airport is immediately obvious, both from the air and from the land. The circular plan efficiently accommodates the circulation of traffic arriving at the airport. It also facilitates the transfer of passengers from one gate to another. Moreover, as the terminal is located in the center of the network of runways, a plane's taxiing time is reduced to a minimum. Passengers disembark at one of the seven satellite terminals that are each equipped to handle half a dozen airplanes simultaneously. Telescopic gangways extend out from these satellites to the aircraft, providing convenient enclosed exit ramps.

Once inside the surprisingly spacious satellite terminal, passengers are struck by a luminous quality, a sense of order and efficiency that accompanies them throughout Roissy. The terminal interior seems absolutely soundproof. Gray and white predominate, highlighted by the orange seating which lends a touch of color to the stark decor. The cosmopolitan atmosphere is emphasized by the mes-

Right, the plan of Charles De Gaulle Airport. The numbers indicate some of the buildings that are ancillary to the central terminal (7):

(1) the commissariat and technical services building. (2) the water tower. (3) the electric power plant. (4) the telephone exchange. (5) the administrative offices. (6) the control tower.

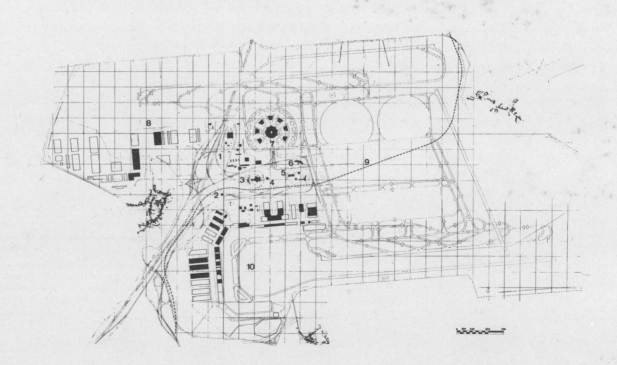

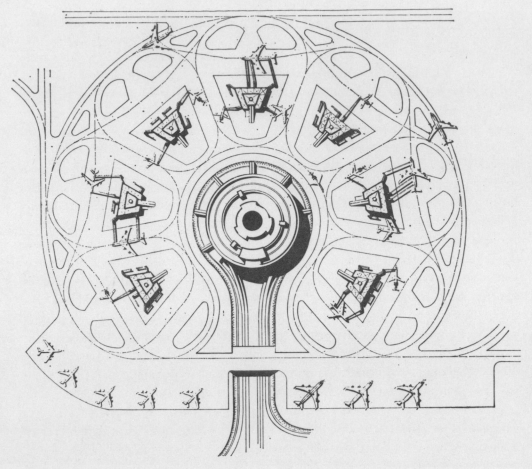

Left, the main terminal at Roissy, Aérogare No. 1, surrounded by its seven satellite terminals. The roadways leading into the center emphasize that the automobile is an integral part of this airport. The chief architect defined Charles De Gaulle as "a place of movement and rest between ground transport and air transport." The diagram reveals the circular concept of his overall design.

Right, the baggage sorting area in the underground level of the main terminal.

Including two underground levels, the terminal building is eleven stories high. The ground-level departure floor contains the ticket counters as well as a cluster of shops and travel services. These vary from chic boutiques to fast-service, duty-free shops, from first-class restaurants to snack bars and newsstands selling international newspapers.

The sophisticated system of handling baggage at Roissy operates, for the most part, out of sight on the lower underground level of the terminal. As soon as luggage is checked in, it is moved automatically, with utmost speed and security. Flight numbers are affixed to each piece, and a centralized computer guides the luggage along a network of conveyor belts and rollers to the basement sorting area. There it is loaded onto a small robot train, controlled by antennae that pick up signals sent out from the central system through wires set in the flooring. The train takes its load along a tunnel and through the appropriate satellite directly to the cargo hold of the plane. The baggage is then simply lifted aboard on pallets.

Above the departure level of the main terminal is the transfer level that leads to and from the satellite terminals and,

sages in many languages that are delivered over the public-address system.

Connecting the satellite terminals with the main building is a futuristic pedestrian circulation system. Paul Andreu, one of the chief architects of Aérogare No. 1, and his associates had been faced with the problem of how to move more than 3,500 people an hour across the nearly 500 feet between terminals—and do it quickly. Their solution was a "travelator." This is a seamless escalator, or mobile floor strip, inside a concrete tube which runs underground and connects the satellites with the main terminal.

Technically the travelator is a tunnel, although this is misleading. The gray walls are made of a tough, but attractive, fibrous

material, brightened by the multilingual illuminated advertisements that blink on and off. Minutes after stepping onto the travelator, passengers are deposited on the outer rim of the main terminal.

Visitors to Roissy are fascinated by their first sight of the main terminal. A glassed atrium separates the outer and inner rings of the building. Beyond this glass—the hole in the center of the bagel—are six transparent tubes piping people from one floor to another, from entrance and ticket counter up to the satellite level and from there farther up to customs. The trip up or down one of these transparent tubes is like a voyage into the future as passengers glide through space and observe fellow travelers passing silently by in other tubes.

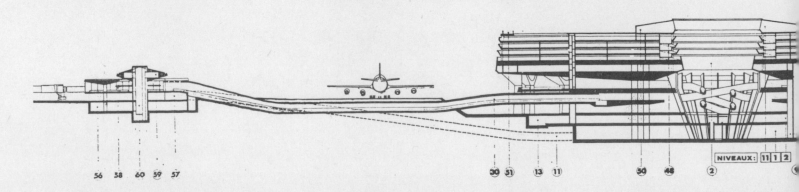

above that, the arrival and customs level. Next up is a floor housing the elaborate technical installations that keep Aérogare No. 1 running smoothly. Above this are four levels for parking, each of which can accommodate 1,000 cars. The building is topped by a roof terrace that commands a clear view out over the airfield to the rolling French countryside beyond.

The entire airport complex—which includes a control tower, a hotel, a water tower, and other facilities in addition to Aérogare No. 1—is bound together by a unity of form and color. Gray, unfaced concrete predominates. This is subtly broken inside the terminals, where the white floor tile with black edging, white furniture with orange upholstery, and green elevator doors provide a suitably unobtrusive background for the variegated crowds.

To leave the airport, passengers cross the arrival-level floor to the road deck that passes in front of the terminal, where they can hail a bus or taxi. The road to Paris dips first under a taxiway and then negotiates a tangle of entrance and exit ramps before connecting with the expressway. It takes thirty minutes at most times—an hour and a half at rush hour—to reach the center of the capital.

The decision to build the airport at Roissy came at a time of economic boom in France. Today this growth has slowed, reducing the demand for a new airport of the scale originally envisioned for Roissy. Moreover, as travel tends toward larger airplanes and fewer flights, Roissy has been left underused.

Roissy highlights the problems that changing economic ambitions can create for a project of this size. On its March 1974

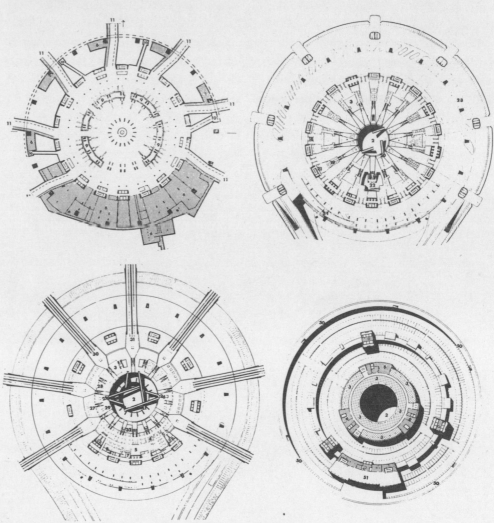

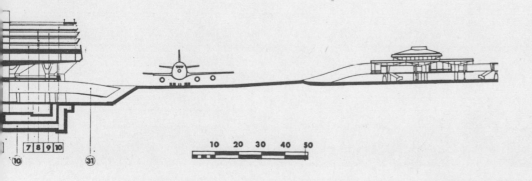

Immediately above, some of the levels of the main terminal in schematic relief (clockwise from upper left): the lowest level used for baggage handling, the departure level, the top parking level with its roof-top viewing terrace, and the mezzanine level from which passengers transfer to the satellites. Left, cross section through the main terminal and two satellites.

opening, the airport was equipped to handle ten million passengers and 400,000 tons of freight a year. Officials projected that, by 1976, the airport would indeed be operating at full capacity. Today, however, only six and a half million passengers and 270,000 tons of freight pass through Roissy each year. In addition to the economic recession, this underuse is due to the often greater convenience of the other airports serving Paris, Orly and Le Bourget.

By 1990, a second terminal complex at Roissy is scheduled to be completed. It was originally expected that the airport would then be handling thirty million passengers yearly. To accommodate these numbers, the construction of a second—and eventually a third—terminal similar to Aérogare No. 1 was planned. However, because of the different economic climate and the reduction in demand, plans have changed. Instead of a circular terminal—whose advantage is in the concentration of services for both incoming and departing passengers—officials are leaning toward a more conventional, linear design. In this form, Aérogare No. 2 could be developed in phases, according to the current need for airport space.

The logical and efficient movement of passengers at Roissy today is a triumph of the technological imagination of the twentieth century. Its designer Paul Andreu claims that, "The vocation of the airport is to be thronged with people from all over the world moving about in every possible direction." This vocation has already been realized at Roissy, even if on a somewhat less ambitious scale than originally envisioned. Fifteen years of environmental, aeronautical, and psychological testing and planning went into Charles De Gaulle Airport. The result is a rational, international transportation center, which goes beyond the pride in the past that prompted its name and expresses France's best hopes for the next century.

A special committee which included a number of local residents promoted the interests of neighboring communities during every step of the planning of the airport. Even now there is active local concern about keeping Roissy clean, quiet, and safe. Below left, a mobile unit monitors air and noise pollution. Screens located around the taxiing area (bottom) deaden noise and detect exhaust. Immediately below, a test stand where engines can run up to full throttle after maintenance work has been done.

Olympia Park

Munich

As host to the 1972 Olympic games, Munich built the ambitious public complex known as Olympia Park, comprising not only stadiums and sports areas but also housing and facilities for athletes, visitors, and broadcasters. The immense and costly project, designed by Behnisch and Partners, was beleaguered by problems and passed through many agonizing revisions, but the end result is a memorable artificial landscape dominated by the controversial roofs of the sports hall, swimming hall, and main stadium—"the largest tent in the world" (preceding page). These daring roofs, designed by Frei Otto, became a symbol of German technology—just as the games themselves symbolized the po-

litical rehabilitation of Germany after the shameful 1936 Olympics in Berlin.

Above, the Olympia Park as it appeared at the time of the games (counterclockwise from the top right) showing the Olympic Village, the Press Center (now a college of physical education), the roof over the sports hall, and the swimming hall with its temporary stands. The fluid, sinuous roofscape (right and below) successfully integrates the sports complex and its pedestrian areas with the gentle contours of the park-like setting.

Top far left, the restaurant, observation, and microwave levels of the broadcast tower. Center far left, the Olympic flame. Remaining plates show the main stadium. The playful and airy curves of the roof create a feeling of movement that complements the activity below. All utility and changing rooms are underground, so that the space remains as open as possible.

In contrast with traditional buildings, which depend on rigidity and gravitational loads for stability, the tent roofs of the Munich stadiums depend on tensile stress. Only the slender, mastlike pylons (top far left) are in compression—the acrylic membranes which form the roof are supported by a fabric of steel cables in tension. The curvatures of the membrane, which seem so freely expressive, are mathematically calculated (left and bottom far left).

The stadiums are illuminated by lights balanced—like birds on a telephone wire—on the main support cables of the roofs (top). Far left center, the swimming hall. Although enclosed, it appears to blend with the landscape outside while reflecting the tent above. Immediately above, the Olympic Village, seen beyond the swimming hall.

The expensive, smoke-colored acrylic panels, ten-foot squares, which form the roof (this page, center right) lie on a supporting layer above the cable. In the words of one critic, "one cannot help thinking that the roof is inside out." Television companies, which contributed a large part of the revenue for the games, insisted on a translucent material, so that the deep shadows detrimental to color broadcasting might be minimized. Regrettably, the panels are not guaranteed to last more than fifteen years.

Form follows function in these views of tent poles, guy ropes, anchors, and canopy (these pages). Right, the front edge of the stadium roof, held in place by five parallel cables. Immediately below and bottom right, the main strut supporting the entrance canopy. The loop formed by the cable enables the stress of all the cables in the fabric to be picked up individually rather than concentrating them at one point.

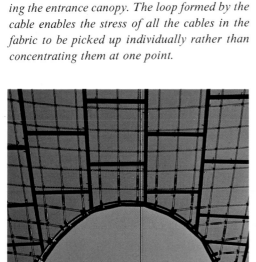

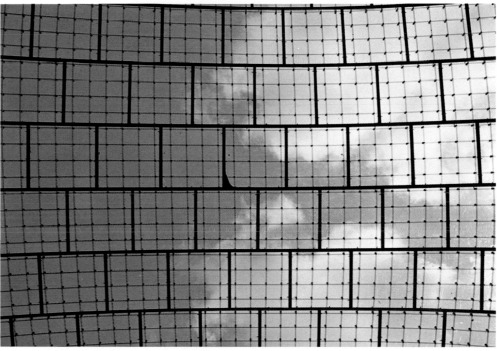

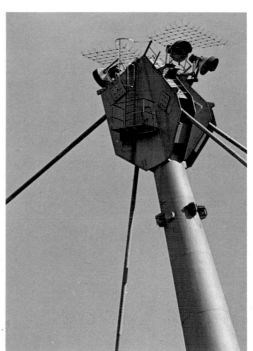

Olympia Park Munich

The 1972 Olympic games in Munich, Germany, were enveloped in tragedy. The idealistic international athletic event was abruptly darkened when a group of Arab terrorists murdered eleven Israeli athletes. The distasteful decision to continue the games on schedule, as though nothing had occurred to dampen the spirit of festivity and brotherhood, had the unfortunate effect of dramatizing the tragedy.

The macabre horror was compounded by a bitter irony. Those with longer memories recognized the Munich games as an effort by Germany to dispel the embarrassing ghost of the display of racist propaganda which characterized Hitler's 1936 Berlin Olympics. As Willi Daume, the president of the organizing committee, commented: "It is to be hoped that the Munich games will expunge impressions that have been prejudicial to Germany's good name ever since 1936."

In keeping with this spirit, Munich organized the biggest, most expensive Olympic games in history. They were the first to be dominated by technology—the first to be televised to all parts of the world throughout their two-week duration. In honor of the games, the center of Munich was restored and cleaned; the airport, subway, and traffic systems were expanded and modernized. But the major undertaking, of course, was Olympia Park—a complete recreational and residential minicity, only minutes from downtown Munich, which was to be the site of the games themselves. The crowning achievement of this thirty-five-acre complex was a monumental sequence of tent roofs, conceived by the architect of the park, Gunther Behnisch and engineered by Frei Otto.

This daring structure has received its share of criticism. Too often, critics have denounced its extravagant cost rather than evaluated the ingenuity and quality of its design. But great works of art have always stirred the imagination, and even observations volunteered by those opposed to the roof are vividly turned. One critic said it looked "from the air like a discarded polyethylene bag;" another likened it to "some grotesque insect impaled on the setting board;" others reduced it to "an immense sheet of gelatin."

One of the more severe disparagements

compared the roof to a beautiful jade burial suit which had recently been excavated in China: "Both are obviously prestigious, expensive, and fascinating, but what justification does either have?" Gunther Behnisch countered the ethical and aesthetic assault with the comment, "In our spiritual world financial problems are not of very great importance."

During the five years which preceded the 1972 Olympics, the burgeoning city of Munich became a huge building site. The

Behnisch's winning design for Olympia Park was founded on a commitment to integrating the installations with the environment. Reading top to bottom, left to right, these preliminary plans show: a schematic drawing of the site's relation to central Munich; the site as it looked in 1967 (the diagonal line is a canal); the new water additions; the area transformed by adding land fill; conventional land fill; conventional types of stadiums required by the Olympic games; the relationship between the three stadiums and the landscape without the roof; a cross section showing how the grandstand and roof forms blend the stadiums with the landscape; a drawing illustrating the complementary nature of the roofs and the sculpted hills; diagrammatic cross sections of the sports hall, the swimming hall with its temporary Olympic bleachers, and the swimming hall without the bleachers.

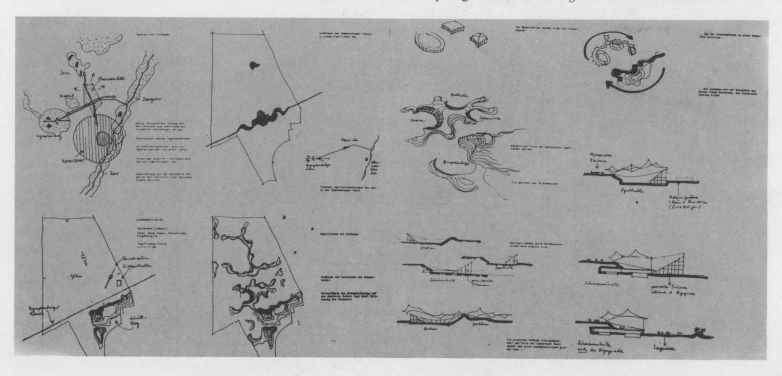

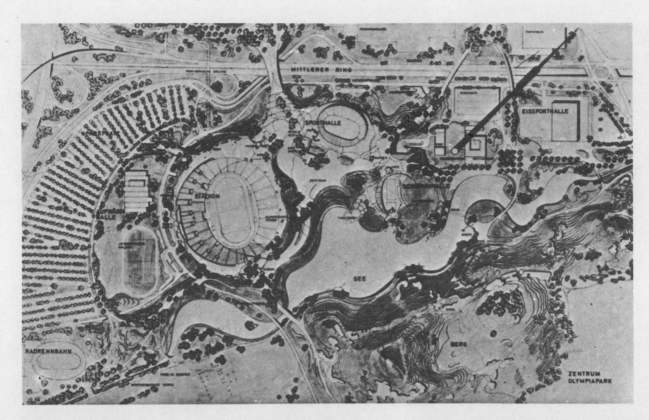

Left, a detailed plan of Olympia Park showing Behnisch's new stadiums (stadion, sporthalle, schwimmhalle); a cycle stadium (radrennbahn); an existing ice stadium (eissporthalle); lake (see); and a new highway.

Below left, a relief model depicting the center of Olympia Park. Below, a relief model of a temporary self-service restaurant and beer garden, one of the relatively few facilities dismantled after the games.

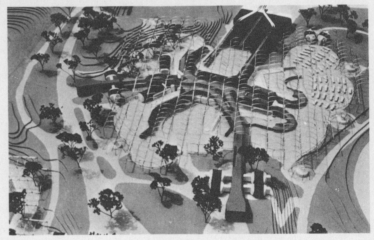

games became the impetus for a vast urban renewal program involving a total of 550 architects, 400 construction companies, and 5,000 workers. The plans for the Olympic complex itself were organized around three slogans: "Olympics in Green," "Olympics of Short Distances," and "Athletics and Art." These catch phrases reflected the problems experienced in previous games held in Rome, Tokyo, and Mexico City, which in various ways had been disorganized and often uninspired in their settings. The designers of the Munich Olympia Park hoped to learn from—and avoid—the unfortunate failings of their predecessors.

The site of the park was the Oberweisenfeld, a former airfield almost two and a half miles north of the city center. Before construction began in 1967, this field resembled an immense urban vacant lot—ugly and flat except for scattered heaps of urban debris from the bombings of World War II at the southern end. This desolate wasteland was to be turned into a single unified landscape that would provide almost all the required facilities for athletes and spectators: various permanent stadiums, a park, and a pocket city—the Olympic Village—to house the visiting athletes during their two-week stay. After the games, these accommodations would become luxury condominiums and student apartments for some 10,000 people.

Behnisch and Partners conceived the project as a total work of art. Their primary objective was to make the three huge stadiums into an integral part of the sculpted green landscape, submerged and molded into the flowing lines of the natural elements of the park. The excavation of the stadiums, the manmade lake, and a new subway line provided earth to cover the small mountain of war debris already on the site and to create a series of hills extending from it. Supporting installations—snack counters, phone booths, ticket kiosks, and dressing rooms—were specially designed as "furniture" for this landscape. At every step, the architects emphasized the human dimension, incorporating hundreds of details meant to encourage spontaneous activities.

The highly controversial tensile roofs were intended to unify the main stadium, the indoor sports hall, and the swimming hall into a single, large form. This, together with the mountain, the lake, and the television tower rising up from the center of the park, was to constitute the Olympic Center. In the eyes of their creators, the roofs were the jewel in the crown of a project already impressive for its scale and harmony. Thus, the Olympics became a perfect opportunity to demonstrate German technological superiority to every television viewer in the world.

The technical problems associated with a tensile structure the size of the stadium roofs were widely considered almost insurmountable—at least within the available time. Frei Otto's canopy for the German pavilion at Expo '67 in Montreal, the largest roof of its kind built before the 1972 Olympics, had sheltered one-tenth of the 800,000-square-foot area Behnisch proposed to cover. Although the ambitious proposal of Behnisch and Partners was chosen from a field of more than a hundred designs, many, including the judges of the competition, regarded Behnisch's idea as a beautiful but impractical flight of fancy.

Even after awarding Behnisch and his collaborators first prize in the competition, the Olympic building authorities considered giving the actual commission to an architect with a more conventional, and presumably cheaper, solution. After heated debate, Behnisch's overall plan, save for the roof, was approved on March 1, 1968. It wasn't until four months later that his plan for the roof, too, was reluctantly accepted.

Consultant Frei Otto's empirical methods of design—which involved solving structural problems with a series of precise models—proved too slow for the harried architects. Engineering, architectural, and electronics experts had to be called in, and the size of the design team grew daily. Advanced computer systems hummed around the clock, solving sets of problems with as many as 10,500 unknowns.

The cost of the design for the stadium roofs alone was said to be greater than that of any building in history—perhaps an extreme demonstration of Behnisch's belief that "intellectual expenditure should take precedence over material expenditure." Yet even as construction on the site began, the ultimate shapes and forms of the buildings were still undetermined. The uncertainty resulted in a great deal of wasted work; in fact, some of the foundations were never used and have been simply buried and landscaped over.

The roof itself is composed of steel cable netting suspended from huge tubular columns between 167 and 283 feet high. This frame is covered with a skin of translucent acrylic plastic. The choice of material for the roof membrane was not made until July 1970, when the television companies—which had agreed to assume a substantial portion of the costs of the Olympiad—insisted that their sensitive color cameras required a tinted, translucent material. This acrylic, unfortunately, is guaranteed to last no more than fifteen years.

In the end, the largest tent in the world

Right, cross section (top) and longitudinal section (bottom) of the enclosed Sports Hall. The playing field lies below the outside ground level, and the terraces of the amphitheater rise to meet the surrounding terrain.

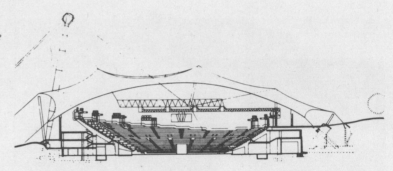

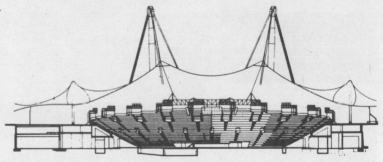

Below, a scale model of the "star wave," one of many roof designs considered and ultimately rejected.

cost eleven times more than its original estimate of 15 million marks—ten percent of the cost of the entire Olympia Park project. Frei Otto himself is said to have remarked wryly that everyone using the athletic center over the next twenty years could have been more cheaply served by free umbrellas and sunglasses.

In their original winning design for Olympia Park, Behnisch and Partners had included proposals for the athletes' housing on the northern half of the site. But the commission appointed the firm of Heinle, Wischer and Partners, which had won third prize in the competition, as architects for these residential buildings, thus leaving Behnisch more time to concentrate on the main stadiums.

Plans for housing were of necessity far more pragmatic. First, the accommodations would have to house 12,000 athletes for two weeks. Afterward, the buildings would be sold as condominiums. So while the athletic stadiums were viewed as a national monument to German avant-garde technology, the housing designs had to conform to rigorous German building codes. Because of the high costs incurred, many of the proposed amenities—including swimming pools, small shopping centers, and open spaces—had to be sacrificed. Though the urban skyline of the precast-concrete residential area contrasts starkly with its green surroundings, the graceful sequence of stadium roofs dominating Olympia Park seems at peace with the undulating countryside. It is hard to forget, however, that in the Olympic Village, not far from the magnificent stadiums, stands a far less imposing stone bearing the names of the Israeli athletes whose deaths only briefly interrupted the 1972 Olympic games.

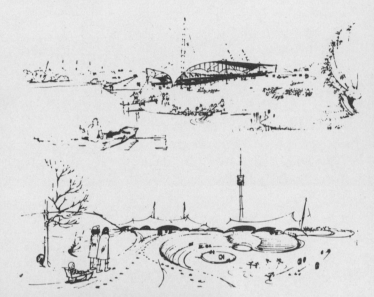

Olympia Park is dominated by a 220-foot landscaped hill (above left) constructed mainly from rubble brought here after the World War II bombings of Munich. The artificial lake at the foot of the hill was formed by widening an existing canal. It is intended for recreational use in both summer and winter (above).

Left, the closing ceremony of the Munich Olympics on September 10, 1972, held under the lights of the main stadium.